D1578400

9112000364738

MOMENTS OF SIGNIFICANCE

A MEMOIR

Shauna O'Briain

First published in the United Kingdom by:
OWN IT! Entertainment Ltd

Company Registration Number: 09154978

Cover Concept: Jason Morgan
Cover Design & Illustration: James Nunn

ISBN: 9780995458956

WWW.OWNIT.LONDON

Dedicated to
My three siblings who have shared this journey with me

The Funeral

I didn't want to go. My mind was finding any excuse to run away. All the Irish family were over to say goodbye to my mum; I weren't ready to say goodbye. The grief thick, family felt like strangers: the bond still present, love flowed, yet I wanted to shut down. I turned up at their hotel; we all went for a meal. I put on a brave face and a steel door to my emotions. In less than 24 hours her body would be cremated.

Laughter and happiness at this reunion – a family long ago torn apart by the ravages of abuse, now united by the grief of the loss of a sister, a daughter, a mother who drunk her life to its end. At first I didn't want to go, but later I didn't want the night to end: in the warmth of the family I could pretend we were here to say hello and not goodbye. The family had been supportive and financially very kind – as Mum didn't have a penny to her name, without that support me and my siblings would have been left with debts on top of the pain.

My sister and I got ready in the morning, purple dresses with black accessories: we thought Mum wouldn't have wanted everyone in black; she was full of colour. We reflected her rebellious spirit with our attire. I looked like a ghost, the shock of loss draining the colour from my face. My sister and I on the street at 9am on the top of Kentish Town Road, close to Tufnell Park: we had matching dresses and heels, received dirty looks from groups of girls, beeps and wolf whistles from vans; the streets an insensitive place to be.

We waited for her body to arrive in the car, which Grandad insisted we follow to the chapel. Once in the car, we bickered and caught jokes. This was the perfect relief from the reality that we were following our mother's dead body.

Arriving at the crematorium, it seemed like my brother weren't going to be one of the pallbearers. I encouraged him to carry his mother's body; that is what men do and he was a man now.

The sun was shining: it was a beautiful September day. I could see best friends past and present; family everywhere. I didn't know who to stand with – not that it was even important in that moment – but that was all I could think of. I wanted the ground to open up and swallow me: so clichéd, yet the clichéd emotion was more welcome than the responsibility of communicating to anyone.

The men of the family carried the coffin into the chapel: my dad, Uncle Sean, two brothers plus Aunty Cathleen's two boys. Tears flowed. Brian wore his as diamonds, glistening on his cheeks. I cried from the depths of my soul: my heart had never been broken like this.

We entered the chapel with Christy Moore's 'Ride On' playing in the background. Moore was one of Mum's favourite singers. She always talked about when she played tin whistle with him when she was 12 – probably some bullshit story, but to her that was her truth and she loved it.

The coffin lay open. She looked different to when I had first identified her body. She was swollen and her face had started to decompose: it was like it was falling, the skin had become so loose; her lips looked all puffed up like a celebrity who has had too many filler injections. The family took turns kissing her; I was thinking Fuck that, I was scared, her face was proper cold. Stroking her hair, I thought, there isn't a soul in that body. They had known her longer than I had, they loved her body more than I did, but I was her child and that's a whole other level of a bond.

I saw my brother at the back of the chapel. I took his hand, and brought him to her. We shared some tears, mixed with family love. We sat down in the front row on the left, right in front of the coffin; Mum's pics smiling at us. The Irish family was on the other side, and some of the neighbours were there too.

I was the first to speak. I had written a piece called, 'The good side of my mum'. Most of my writing had been full of anger, so I was thankful I had taken the time to reflect on the good times 'cause it had prepared me in advance for this moment. I felt proud to be sharing my writing with her: I knew her spirit could hear me; I could feel her all around me.

Aunty Cathleen went next, sharing stories of all the mischief they would get up to in Ireland as kids. Aunty Cathleen was only about a year older than my mum. They were best friends, always out on adventures; even up until Mum passed they were still close. The stories warmed my heart.

4 Non Blondes' 'What's Up' was the next song to play: this was me and Mum's tune. I would sing the harmonies for her. In my head I heard Mum say, 'Sing for feck sake would ya?'

We sang out loud along to the song. For a moment, I was transported back to the kitchen in my childhood, with her playing on her guitar; but I snapped back to the present, where we were saying goodbye to her life.

Lucy stood up. We met Lucy when she was 14 – she had run away and our family took her in. Mum and Lucy shared a strong bond: we are the same age and Mum saw her as a daughter; good thing really as mine and Mum's relationship had broken down. Lucy shared a beautiful piece, full of heart and emotion. Grandad spoke. He got onto his knees, took out his beads and said the rosary. It was a relief to a lot of the family to see him, 87 years old and still going strong, even though his voice cracked with the emotion of losing his daughter as he prayed aloud.

Next my brother shared a piece on Mum having to be both mum and dad to us. I was proud of him for standing in his truth and honouring his mum in her final moments. Our dad shared a reading from the Bible. James Taylor's 'Fire and Rain' played as the coffin passed through the curtains to be cremated. The coffin got jammed and took a minute to go through; stubborn Mum to the last minute.

I said goodbye as the coffin left us. Me, my brothers and sister sobbed in floods, unaware of the other people in the room.

Finally the Levellers came on, 'Another Man's Cause': she loved this song.

As we sat in our sorrow and grief, the doors to the chapel opened and the sun streamed through from a gorgeous garden outside.

Afterwards, people came up to me and said that the minute I started to speak at the lectern earlier in the service, I was bathed in white light. It was magical, so I was told. It offered some comfort: I thought it was you, Mum, still shining onto my body, with the light from your soul.

Home

Every evening at dinner was a walk on eggshells – if we got dinner that is, 'cause our mum would get drunk and forget she had hungry teenagers to feed.

Mum had around seven different personalities, and you would never knew which one you would get. Her reaction to conversation would be different depending on her mood. Clash with one of her sides on the wrong day and it was raining dishes in the kitchen – a downpour of china – splintering and shattering in succession; her red hair blazing, eyes alive like she was possessed. The smashing and screaming would normally come after school had finished. We'd be at the dinner table, confused. The floor covered in shards, with no way to walk, nowhere to go. She would say to her boyfriend Andy that she needed a drink. He was cool: I liked that one. He would get her some drinks, though this would usually end with us all feeling fucked, the shattering of the plates breaking parts of us; pieces of childhood innocence smashed into fragments that got swept into the bin.

I would clash with Mum. I would push her a lot of the time. Dunno why I wanted to do that, push her until she attacked. I was the red rag and she was the bull. I would get in her face until she went for me. Did I find love inside of the violence? Was that my safe space? Was that the attention I wanted, the reason why I pushed at her?

When she would go for me it was full on: never a small beating, always a rage. Before school she would say she was going to hit me so hard I wouldn't sit down for a week. I remember picturing myself at school not being able to sit down 'cause my bum was bruised.

The wooden spoon was her favourite. It would be a dance between smacks. The hiding would last for at least 20 minutes, me screaming 'Don't hit me': she was deaf when the violence was inside of her. I remember me and my brother being so young – I was not even five – and receiving a full hiding. Worst of all was when she said, 'Go get the wooden spoon', making me get the item that I would be beaten with myself. Afterwards, I would pull down my pants, looking at her handprint and marks on my bum: red, big, sore. I felt sorry for myself, yet I never had the fear of the beating coming – not enough to stop me vexing her again.

One time, on the way home from school, it was raining and she slipped over. I laughed: it was funny. That was it. I was in for it. Got home, had to pack my bags to go to foster care. I was six years old.

I packed my bag ready to leave. I took my poster – a felt colouring poster – and kept imagining it in my new room. In the end I was sent to my dad's for a few days. I had genuinely thought I was leaving the family for foster care. This would become a regular threat; the threat of being sent to foster care. My siblings would cry and beg for me to be allowed to stay.

Over the years, things escalated, until one day my mum grabbed my hair, dragged me to my room across the floor with my head smashing on every door. In those moments I wanted to fight back, but my love was so strong it felt wrong to hit my mother, so this was now normality, her bull-raging. She would sit across my body: I would beg, scream, cry, plead, and she would slap my face and restrain my arms on the ground. She would bite and scratch me, bang my head off walls, though nothing that left any noticeable marks – not where people could see them anyway.

Life was getting progressively worse: school was a big haze, and home life was like watching out for hidden mines under the floorboards, unexpected explosions awaiting, depending on Mum's moods and how drunk she was: maybe happy drunk; maybe violent drunk. She was constantly threatening to get rid of me, getting my blanket, pictures – everything I loved – then throwing them out of the window onto the nasty estate. She would rip up my work, my poems… Her words were swords of torture that cut through all the hope I had for my life.

I wished I had the guts to end it all, but looking around my room and my little sister's stuff – her toys and the young life yet to find its way – I knew I had to be there; her warrior in this war. I would run out of the flat into the dark night, nowhere to go, and stop by the bins at the bottom of the block and sob, a waterfall of emotions; the pain like knives cutting through my chest. Lost in the concrete jungle. Because I had nowhere to go I would have to go back 'home', whatever that is, that place… where my bed was like a bed of nails: uncomfortable and dangerous.

Emotionally hungover in the mornings before school, eyes puffed out, the weight of the world on my shoulders, feeling trapped and at the same time wanting to be a 'normal' teen and fit in with the girls at school, it felt like I was walking on quicksand: nothing was solid. I could be sucked into the unknown at any moment, and the teachers were talking about getting good grades for my GCSEs. None of that shit related to any part of my life, yet I wanted so badly to be that fantastic student.

I was an outcast, 14-years-old, hormones raging through my body. Mum would blank me for days after an argument. I didn't know how to find a way out of these situations: the house a thick fog of anger, smoking hash in the blocks every night. I could see the whole of London from the top of the block, the twinkling lights of others' lives. I would see the radius of the estate and wonder what happened outside of that place, 'cause we were in hell right then, but once I was high I didn't care too much; a nice big cushion against reality. The stars twinkled in the night sky. It was cold so whoever was present huddled around the joint – puff puff give… I blazed with the boys 'cause I didn't like the girls much. The blocks were our home 'cause the flats we lived in felt colder than the winter night.

I started to run away after school, going to a friend's house and not letting Mum know where I was and getting friends to not let their mums call my mum. I wanted her to know what it would feel like to lose me, to know what it would be like if I didn't come home. One time, I hid at a friend's. Her mum got home late and got me to call my mum. I was so scared a beating was gonna happen 'cause there was bad blood the night before. She was up and drunk when I got in and she didn't say a thing to me. She hugged and kissed me in front of all her friends that she had invited back from the pub. I shuddered in confusion, then joined in with the party, puffed some of the hash and necked some beer.

She was the woman I loved most in the world: she was so abusive, yet I always craved her love so deeply. She was my queen: I would write her love poems and beg to be forgiven after our fights. I wanted to see her smile, to have those perfect moments that made life shine with the sun of happiness; waiting for the spring flowers to emerge from this frost.

Love

We all want love. It is sold in the most beautiful packages: it is sold in films as all that matters in life; that having a mate means success; that marriage is success; that we should all aim for the 2.4 children, a perfect family. I've always been a rebel and maybe that's because I have never experienced any real love stories in my life – tragedies, yes. I now work on not being limited by my history and am taking the road of re-learning what love is. Romantic Love is not a magical answer to unhappiness. Romantic Love is not an answer to any of my problems. Romantic Love is not easy.

Love keeps chipping away at my perceptions of what love is; chipping away at my ego and the stories I have built around who I think I am; removing the filter that's over my life; making me lose the glasses through which I could only see the past in my present; allowing me to see with new eyes. I see this moment as it is now. I let love show me what is in my world right now.

My last big love and relationship was eight years ago. I had the deepest sexual connection I had ever had, with this woman. I dreamed of her for a few solid years after we split up. Every night I would dream of kissing her, and wake up to each new day sweating and anxious at the reality of life without her. I thought she was the only woman I would ever feel this for.

We had eight months of having hours of sex each day; not working much, just being totally into each other while letting all of the other joys of life slip us by. We made music and supported each other's lives. We had slipped into the euphoria created by sharing our bodies: it was beyond orgasmic; it was inter-dimensional, deep and full of pain. Our souls danced in a divinity, in a space beyond this realm: she was my love.

We split up, but still saw each other and fucked wherever we could. It turned into a game – me asking her to leave me alone, to leave me, to blank me, to move away. This created so much tension and sexual energy: a volcano waiting to explode. We would hold it for as long as we could but it so often ended in an earth-shattering orgasm, naked in bliss, then cold with the knowledge that we only felt connected and in love when we were having sex. I thought this meant we were meant to be together, the reality was we were not together; only sex connected us in moments. The sexual energy was profound: I felt love and that she was the love of my life. She was able to have sex with me, then go off and have fun, to fuck other girls, to explore the gay scene. I knew she needed to do that as I had already been through that part of my journey. I felt like I should try not to hold her or make her mine. If we were meant to be, she would return to my life and we would reconnect to the love.

When we started to come to the end of our affair – just when I realised I had to stop telling her that I weren't into this any more, and properly move on and show it with my actions – my mum died. The biggest love I ever had was for my mum. With her passing away, I knew heartbreak like I had never known before. First heartbreak from the woman I had thought was my greatest love, then the loss of the woman that really was. My body became an icicle: no feeling, no emotions. It felt like the whole world was to blame. Happy couples smiling all around me, I felt like an outcast once more. I could never have what they did; I was too far gone with pain. I ended up back in her arms and her knickers within a couple of days. She was with me at Mum's funeral; we slept together afterwards. I would tell myself lies, not bothering to think about what we were doing and what it really meant. But then she found her way to a friend of mine – one of the lesbians in my circle, a bit of a rival. To lose my mum, then watch the woman I thought was The One begin a relationship with a top dyke from the scene? Every part of my heart screamed in pain. I went into shutdown. Emotionally and sexually, it all became rather dark for me. I lived in a headspace of my own. I no longer attracted women the way I used to: my pain was a woman repellent.

*****

A year after this, I had a very beautiful lover for a few weeks. She was younger and we were in such different places in our lives. I felt blessed by our connection: we sweetened each other's path with sex-love, yet our roads led in separate directions soon after.

A few months later, two years after Mum passed, I ended up back in the throes of sex with Her, the one I thought was The One. Back to her: back to black. It all happened out of the blue. I guess it was never finished with her; we needed one more experience to close the chapter. It was unfortunate that our sexual connection was behind her girlfriend's back. And the sex was so good. It was beyond sex; it was an orgasmic communication of our souls. How could we create so much magic then not be together? How could this be love, and why did it hurt so much?

My body completely shut down again after it ended (again). I could have beautiful women in my bed and feel absolutely nothing. Afterwards I would cry as if I was crying out every bit of pain in my soul. It ached and it hurt. I just wanted to be 'normal', to be able to make love, have sex and connect. During dates I couldn't make a move: I had lost my spark, my mojo.

For two years I was on my own – no hugs, no one sharing my bed, no friends staying over, no kisses; just the bitterness of trying to find a way through the grief. The sexual frustration was like fire running across my skin, burning all my hairs and leaving me feeling singed, hairless and unattractive. Everyone else around me seemed to be able to create a life of happiness in couples. I felt like I was totally alone: why couldn't I create what they had created?

I tried to change the way I was thinking and behaving, but then I'd reflect all the hate I had for myself onto my environment. It felt like everyone else's fault. I would chant, and ask how I had created this situation; I'd become determined to make a change but would still end up back in a world of self-loathing. I would try and be close to women unsuccessfully: no one is attracted to a desperate energy. The rejections from women due to my closed energy, led to me feeling less able to open up – a vicious cycle.

*****

Eventually, something inside me told me I had to go to the Bliss festival in Thailand. It was a mission to get there but I made it just in time: I found love in paradise on a perfect beach, on a perfect island, with a goddess – flame-red hair, soft freckles... She was the goddess of all the magic at that festival. We kissed the first night we met, in a hammock, with the stars as our blanket and the sea our soundtrack. We glimpsed heaven: she showed me that love could exist for me again. We spent New Year's together: four days of bliss and we had yet to sleep together. She walked me home in the dark each night; we kissed on the porch as the sand tickled our toes. We saw in the New Year with a kiss and my heart had a glimmer of hope. When she left, I travelled eleven hours to where she lived in Thailand before returning home. We made beautiful love that night. It felt so good to sleep in her arms. After two years of being celibate, I was beginning to open up again.

I invited her to move to London with me. I sent her love letters, I sent her poems and songs. She blanked me out. I just kept pushing without any response. In my mind she was gonna come to London; in reality she weren't coming anywhere. It had been a holiday romance in the most perfect setting. At the time I blamed her and couldn't see why she didn't want to come and be with me. Reality had blurred, and I had wished for her to be the answer to all that was causing me pain.

If my outer life was a reflection of my inner world, then what was I reflecting? A deep sense of non-existent self-love and a belief that I was not strong enough to work through heartbreak again. I dug deeper in prayer and self-reflection. I also had some therapy. I looked at the raw truth of my inner reality and faced the life of the image I had created for myself; I saw the ugly side of me I wanted to ignore while feeling its wrath in my life.

After such an abusive upbringing with my mum, I had a deep belief that I was unloveable. It fucking hurt and it was so lonely to face the truth. I started to work on negative thoughts: I'd think, 'I am unattractive', then say to myself, 'Actually, I think I'm at least, like, alright-looking and a nice person, so why can't I attract a woman?'

Through my Buddhist practise, I started to heal these thoughts, to sit with them while I chanted, and to transform them. I watched my reality transform in front of my eyes.

I opened up to the thought that sex could be an incredible tool for healing – that there were beautiful women out there I could connect with who would be open to healing together with me, through the realm of touch. I started to do online dating and attracted a lover into my life. My ghetto chick, she linked me in some rundown pub in some ruff endz. I was opening up to other possibilities and not the ideas of perfection my ego had created. I went back to her place and she put on the TV. I'd not watched it in years. I worked on holding back my judgment. We kissed and it was electric; we caught a real nice vibe.

We would link for sex: it was respectful, sensual, intimate. We would sleep naked, wrapped in each other's arms, then wake up early to have more sex. It ended with respect. We still spoke for a while until we were ready to move on: we both wanted more but knew we weren't the ones to give it to each other.

I learnt not to make every girl I had good chemistry with 'The One'. I had a very gorgeous stream of wonderful women that I became lovers with, in two years of dating and exploring. Each woman showed me an element of what it was I really wanted in a partner; each reflected a part of me that needed deep healing.

I dated women I would not usually date; I had incredible

dates and wonderful conversations. And I respectfully drew the connections to a close when the time for being together had passed. I treated women with the respect I wished I could have been treated with, meeting in person to move on, even if it had been a short connection. I hated confrontation, to have to face my life head-on, literally. I saw this new way of being as freedom from the conditioning of my ego, which had made up so many rigid rules, and which had caused me so much suffering. Each encounter was a blessing – an opportunity to grow as a person and to expand my heart; to heal through touch; to play and explore.

It was uncomfortable at the end of each connection, regardless of who ended it, but I went through it each time without judgment, knowing that I could have more and that there was more out there for each of us.

Yet it's funny how I could think I had healed but still be so blocked.

I met a woman. She was a princess, looked like a Disney character: she was so beautiful. We got intimate the first couple of times we met, I felt a depth of connection like I had not felt in a very long time. She disappeared then reappeared a few months later. She wanted to take it slow; so slow we didn't even kiss. We would stroke before we went to sleep – and we slept a few nights a week together, half-naked, wrapped around each other all night. I would go to sleep feeling so horny and frustrated, yet I felt loved so I didn't question it; I kept exploring.

After around six weeks I couldn't do it any more: after being out, I'd want to make sweet love to her, to express all I had been feeling all day. She weren't ready. So we decided to go back to being friends. I didn't blame her for not wanting to be sexual. I looked at myself and asked myself what was really going on. I reflected on our connection and it hit me: ooooh she was a manifestation of the frustrated energy I was still carrying. I thought that I had healed yet I was attracting love like this. I still held, deep within me somewhere, the notion that my sexuality was not beautiful.

So I learned to let that go and decided that the way I make love is beautiful; that I could attract such a gorgeous lover into my life. I had to keep going deeper into how I viewed myself, how I felt about myself, because my outer life was a mirror of my inner.

The tables turned: the girls I dated made such beautiful efforts and showed so much affection. Still, the magic was always missing. I told the universe that I could have it all: I could have my best friend, amazing lover and all-round awesome woman – all in one woman. Most importantly, I could have magic with that woman. My friends called me fussy, and damn right I'm fussy. I respected every goddess who shared their queendom, but there was more, I knew it: the fussiness was making my vision clear.

*****

After two weeks since my declaration to the universe, she appeared on an app. She looked cute – not my usual type, but I had been more open to different things recently and decided to open up to a new world. We talked all the next day and linked that evening; pretty much record timing for me, connecting online. We met at 7pm on a Saturday night in Camden. I checked her: she was cute, she had curly hair; she weren't too tall. She was smiling and we instantly hugged, which created an atmosphere of ease. We walked through

Camden, my intrigue growing, wanting to sit face to face and to see her properly. The bustling of the streets faded into a blur, and we walked until we could find a place to sit and sip a warm cup of tea. She only had a card – I had cash, so I paid. The man behind the counter called me boss. I'm not the boss: it felt kinda embarrassing, which was annoying as I had just met this woman.

She was beautiful: she smiled lots, she met me in conversation. I felt a spark, a connection, and I knew she was going to be a profound love in my life. I planned my next move, while still paying attention to the conversation. Everyone had left the café and it was just me and her. It was time to leave. I invited her to Primrose Hill; a romantic spot with London's city lights as our backdrop for the evening. It was cold up there. I wanted to wrap myself into her but we weren't close like that, even though she felt so familiar just then. It was getting proper cold. I was chapping – couldn't have kissed her even it had got that far 'cause my teeth were chattering.

We found a pub where we warmed up, sat close – I rubbed her cold hands in mine. There was a spark. I was nervous, so didn't move closer. We moved on, found a cafe to have late-night soup. It was four dates in one. We were on the tube – I brushed her lips with mine for a quick kiss before I jumped off the train. I had just met this woman, yet there was the magic I had been talking about.

We met in the park a few days later. It was a blazing hot day, the first of the year. I wondered how we'd make it to a kiss as the conversation flowed so well. We hid under the sheet I had brought as I had no sunscreen and didn't fancy getting burnt by the sun. We slowly moved closer, we kissed. It was so magical, so full of chemistry; the sun pounding on our heads as we hid from its powerful rays. I knew then that I was going to fall in love that summer. It had taken eight years to understand the feeling and to truly feel it. This woman had shown me that love was in my life: I didn't know just then if it would be with her, as I didn't want to project that onto her, but she had shown me that it was a possibility.

I welcomed that summer of love. The months went by, things got deeper between us, the magic full. She was all I had called for: the friendship, the sex, the magic. We held back from labels and took it fast yet slow, respectful, enjoying the stages of falling in love.

*****

My ex – the one I'd thought was The One – hit me up. She was back from her travels and wanted to hang out. I let my new love know the situation and it led to an uncomfortable discussion. I didn't fully explain the situation to her: I had texted her late at night to let her know that my ex was around and wanted to see me. She stepped back for a few days, still in contact but not around. This was a sharp shift from the woman that made time to see me every day.

While I chanted, I realised that I was ashamed of the fact that I had not been in a relationship since Mum passed away, since my last significant ex; that I was ashamed that the grieving process hit me so hard that my body turned to stone. I had been dating for two years and I had started to open up to love. My heart burned as I saw all the parts of myself I had yet to heal – parts I thought were healed but I now saw were still raw. Why was I ashamed of my years alone? Why did I think that to be a whole person in those years I would have had to have had romance? I could barely love myself then: my world was dark and I had to confront the darkness alone.

I needed to pluck up the courage to let this new, this special person know my 'secret' – that I had been grieving for my mum and my broken childhood for a while; that I was starting to heal; that I was afraid she wouldn't want to be with me when she found out I was 'broken and alone' (as I thought of myself).

All my relationships had been toxic – from those with my parents and the rest of my family, to my relationship with drugs and drink, and my relationships with women. All was a jumbled mess. I had stood back for long enough to spend years unravelling the ball of knots I'd tied myself into. It took time, patience, blood, sweat and tears. I should have been able to stand strong with all I had come through, and acknowledge it was bravery to stand alone in my pain, with my bad habits. I had grown from trauma to be able repeatedly say to myself I deserve more, and despite the story of my past, I can have more.

After two years of dating and eight years alone, I had found someone that I wanted to see and to be with. I get triggered like crazy saying it – the old poison coming to the surface – but this is what I asked for. I had called her into my life.

Love is looking at yourself – the deeper parts the parts of yourself that you struggle to love – so both you and others can love them. In turn, you have a larger capacity to love others. I had a larger capacity to love her.

She came over: we talked; we kissed; she asked about my ex. I gave her the full story: I told her how the relationship had left me physically cold; I told her the story of how ashamed I felt to have been so alone. She kissed me and it felt like nectar to my soul. She made love to me and as I orgasmed, tears flowed from my eyes. She held me, put her hand on my heart. She saw me naked and in pain, she poured love onto the moment.

*****

We had our first clash at a festival. I went to pack and go home, to leave and let her understand that I didn't like where things had got to between us during our argument. I thought that hurting her would make her feel my hurt.

After a day full of tears, I knew I couldn't leave her like that: it would be cruel. I sat with my fear for the day and by the time she got back from her shift, things were calmer. We caught some jokes while packing, then we had a talk on the way home in her car.

We listened to each other; we gave space to each other without judgment. When I heard her side, it made sense. She heard mine, and we understood that we had miscommunicated. This calm talking through of things with her was such a healing experience; to allow each other to be, without being defensive, without trying to change each other's feelings towards the situation. It was beautiful. We grew closer; we learnt that we could move through the uncomfortable spaces between us without putting fuel on the fire, and see things as they truly were. In this hall of mirrors we call life, I faced myself naked as we made love.

My view is that love is healing. Regardless of what future I have with my love, this experience is transforming my heart. I can now see glimmers of a family happening in my life, as the dysfunctional memories are being replaced with love and respect.

I now see….

that love is looking at the parts of oneself that feel unlovable and exposing them to love

that love is respect for my partner's thoughts and feelings that are different to mine

that love is expansive and beyond any of the 'rules' set out by my ego that I am love and that you are love: that we are love.

My Dad

48 years old: 32 of those years as an experienced drug user; 24 years as an addict. Not exactly someone to look up to.

He's small, stocky – well, chubby. His teeth are tiny yellow-brown stubs – the drugs reside there, a reminder of the years of self-abuse. Yet when he looks in the mirror, he sees pearly whites shining back. Makes me wonder: do we ever really see our own reflection?

He tells me tales of his youth – being 16, asking a mate to score him a draw, his friend couldn't get the hash and brought back some heroin instead and they all banged it up. He says he was smashed instantly, gone from this world (he acts out his words with massive hand gestures as he speaks, a proud gleam in his eye). As if this is useful information for my life, some great fatherly advice.

At 16, he always knew he would follow the path of drugs, he says, knew he couldn't be a father. Why become a father? He looks at me while saying these words, his part-creation. I'm just another part of his life to escape when he's chasing the dragon;

his existence on a piece of tinfoil or the tip of a needle. He talks of his power and what he can do. Makes me think of when I took drugs, especially trippy ones. The answer to the whole universe was on those lines of K or tabs of acid. But the next day I still had to get on the bus.

I hear his words and look at his body: holes in his arm, track marks across his entire pale frame; pinhole eyes, pupils so small he's not absorbing much of this world. I realise he's a traveller, a cosmic surfer, realm to realm through his brown adventures. Heroin: more than his mistress; now his master. The power is lost once you're controlled – a need, no longer just a lust.

My father. I have his nose, maybe. I used to love his stories. Intrigued, as a youngster, by the drug experiences he had had. Part of them stories I have written into my own life. I've followed some of the footsteps he left in front of me, as a daughter does a father. I have no memories of him sober. Now he speaks and I think, 'What a load of shit, how can you speak to me'? Only proud when speaking of escaping this world. My sister's house needs painting; your grandchild needs a new bed. I walk into the living room; he's curled up like a little foetus on the floor, hood up. Is that his life? 48 years on earth, trying to return to the womb. He cries 'cause he was adopted: that's why he can't deal with life; a Houdini at escaping this reality.

I miss the dad I never had, sometimes, but I have to wake myself up and give thanks in my heart that he was given life, even while he throws it away. Him doing drugs all his life is part of the reason I spent years fucked up and depressed. To stand next to him – my 28 years to his 48 – and hear him try and speak his victim-talk: I just can't condone it.

I tell him to wake the fuck up. It's like shouting through a room full of fluffy pillows, but I don't stop. I shout, trying to reach his heart: 'Make your children proud of you, make your dead foster-parents proud, make the parents who gave you away proud... DO SOMETHING!!!!' The biggest mind-fuck with having addicts as parents is that, when I see them totally fuck themselves up on drink or drugs, I feel to do what they do, to deal with my pain and rejection using their methods. To visit their drug or drink friend to help me understand why I, the person they gave life to, am not enough for them to want life.

Writing is my saviour, my stick that guides me through my torn soul and broken heart in times when this world feels a little too tough.

Red Jen

I had just turned 21 and moved back to my mum's. I had flipped on a coke binge – some random guy I had met in some late night dodgy bar was feeding it to me; he wanted to fuck me. I so didn't want to fuck him, the drugs messed me up that night. I didn't understand what I was doing with my life and why everything was the way it was. Life was so fucked up: I went to my mum's to try and find home. Instead I found a dark space with drunk people drinking cans of cider for breakfast. My mum and her friends locked themselves in dark rooms 'cause my mum was ashamed of her drinking. I was on the brink, so sick of my life, bored of the way I was living, needing, wanting change for myself. Yet my reality was full of adults who had given up on life through drink and drugs. I had no understanding of how to keep myself happy, just a sense that I could do something more with my life but I didn't really know how.

My aunty Frances had bought me a term of drama lessons at a college as a present, it was a once a week evening class, this had sparked an interest in me. I enrolled in college that September 2001 to do an access course in Community Theatre in Hackney – it looked like a good course. I was at my mum's and thinking there must be a way I can realise my dream of being an actress.

Looking out the window of my mum's flat at the brick houses opposite, looking at the grass park that was once rubble I knew I wanted to make a change here; I wanted to contribute towards creating a brighter space. Silla Carron, the woman who had taken my sister in (even though my sister weren't staying with her any more we were still close), offered me the hall space for free on the estate to run workshops. The first day I opened the hall no kids turned up. I left and went to the library, made some posters and stuck them around the estate, got a book out of the library on drama games and found some workshop ideas. The next week a couple of children turned up and the sessions started.

Silla called Jen. A woman running a local arts orginisation to support young people and let her know there was a young woman she might want to work with. Red Jen as I knew her came to find me in the Clarence Way Estate hall; I was working with a couple of young people. This woman walked in: curly dyed bright red hair, she was mixed raced, dressed in nice jeans like Edwins and checked shirt with red trainers; puma or something close to that.

Jen is a powerhouse full of energy: she is bright, bounces when she talks, and her energy flies through the atmosphere like lightning striking a beam of light out to those in the darkness of the storm. She ran a company called S-Teem, which helped young people to gain self-esteem and confidence through the Arts. I was given space in Jen's office, up at the top of the

Winch Project building in Swiss Cottage, where I could use the computer. Jen would be there, sharing her life with me. She was the first adult other than a social worker I got to work with who was clean from drink and drugs. Jen had stories from her past that were harsher than mine: she had been in foster care, had come from a very dysfunctional home, she had also been a pop star in the 80s with a band called the Belle Stars; an all-female band. She had lived through hell in her childhood to go on to writing hit songs. Her infectious positive attitude started to shake me out of my 'poor me' state of mind and I started to see a light at the end of the long tunnel.

Jen supported me with the running of the drama club, teaching me how to write reports after each session. She gave me a little funding and I got us some circus equipment to learn some new skills with the kids who came to my workshops. She supported me with housing, too: I moved into shared housing after finding a room thanks to the Irish Centre. My mum had always used the Irish Centre, I knew they were good for helping with many issues, I got a room in a shared place in Tottenham. I signed on, so my rent was paid and then started my course at Hackney Community College. Life was looking up.

One mad Irish girl that lived in the house share where I lived wanted to have it out with me one day: she was convinced I had been in her room, which I hadn't. We ended up having a physical fight. The girl ran at me, knocking me over. I jumped up rammed her into the wall then pushed her onto the stairs: I was on top of her, punching her. She was screaming for me to stop – the two boys with her didn't do anything and my mind was reaching a white space but I pulled back, stopped and got up. She stood up and said to the boys, 'If she ever steps to me again I'll put her in hospital.' I was just defending myself: this spot had become my home. I belled Jen as I ran through the Tottenham streets, tears flowing, lump in my throat, so angry; the fight didn't help the anger in fact it made it worse. My world felt like it was crashing as I ran through the high-street to nowhere. Fuck, I had helped the girl to move her friends in and it turned out she was crazy.

Jen came down with her mate George to help me move. He brought his big van with him, which I piled all my stuff into and I moved out that night. I took my little cat with me and went back to my mum's.

I woke early the next day only for my mum to tell me all my stuff needed to be out that night, that there was no space for me at hers. Jen took me to a centre for homeless young people. I had no money, no job and no family to fall back on. I got a spot in the homeless people's hostel that night. The walls of my room were dirty white with blood stains from someone's needle hits of heroin.

Jen helped me stay strong; I found a new home for my cat and got on with it. She was my rainbow, the colours of hope after the storm, painting love onto the grey clouds of my life. If she could get through all she had been through in her life, I could get through mine too. I got a bigger room after a month, which was fortunate as I got my first girlfriend there. I did the best I could. I would phone Jen, mad and upset: she would say, 'Write a poem about it.' I would write all day in my room when I weren't at college, learning to make use of my anger to put to paper the injustices I could see in the world.

I would ring Jen feeling sorry for myself and she would say 'Get your act together.' She was there when I needed strong guidance, strict and firm with love 'cause the self-pity song ain't pretty, plus it can take time to change a tune. I was doing well at college and Jen was training me up to run workshops. We created the lesson plans together; I supported her on projects in schools, youth clubs and community events. She schooled me on how to deliver my poems: I was awful at it. I would rhyme fast 'cause I thought that was how it sounded rhythmical and Jen would always say 'Slow down a bit.' It took me at least ten years to understand.

Jen hooked me up with my first poetry show at Express Excess in Chalk Farm with Paul Lynls. I was paid £15, which was a bus pass for the week and some baccy money for me. A few of my friends from my college came along to support. I got a taste for performing my own work and I liked it. Acting was cool at college but I got too connected to my characters when playing them; performing my own words, sharing my own story and heart resonated so much more.

While living in the hostel I was awarded £5,000 from the Prince's Trust to run a drama project on my estate that summer. I managed to get a Distinction in my course from college. Jen supported and guided me through the whole process. I moved hostels to one with more young people and fewer drug addicts and sex workers. Finally I was managing to grasp at a little more for myself. I loved the women in the hostel. I was just 21 and wanted to find a life outside of being surrounded by drug addiction. It was all I had ever known, but my soul, my spirit knew I could have other experiences: I just had to work real hard to make it happen.

Going to Red Jen's place in Camden, seeing all the gold discs on her wall, the framed pics of her on the front cover of Melody Maker, hearing the stories of her on tour with Madness mixed with the tragic things going on in her life at that time, I realised that the backdrop to success could and did grow from a broken space. Jen was the rose that grew through concrete: I now had someone to look up to, real support, a mentor.

It was Jen who introduced me to spiritual literature, first *The Alchemist* by Paulo Coehlo, then *Conversations With God* by Neale Donald Walsch, and onto *Same Soul, Many Bodies* by Brian L. Weiss. Jen had been saved by the Buddhist monks in Scotland after her partner had committed suicide, and she found her way back to life by volunteering at a woman's charity for refugees: the stories of the women were the jolt of perspective that gave her gratitude for her life. This led to Jen setting up the young people's charity. Lucky me that Jen found her path. She is my spiritual mum: she never had children and we were searching for these roles in our lives: me, the older woman to look up to, and she, the young woman to impart her wisdom and life passion to. It was preordained this meeting; my soul weren't coming to this planet unless I got to meet Jen in this lifetime.

Over the years, Jen has always been there for me. When her niece was murdered in Camden back in 2005, we stood outside the spot where she lost her life on Christmas Eve and decorated the metal gate with flowers and the love from our hearts. We held a cheerful space while we waited for the pastor to do the evening prayers at this tragic spot. Jen stood strong in the face of this tragedy. Her brother had passed just two months prior. How was she still standing? How was she still a bright light for the community and for her family during that cold winter? Each snowflake holds an individual pattern and Jen's snowflake is a diamond; it shines 'cause it grew in the rough, covered in dirt; now it is priceless and unbreakable.

We don't communicate as much as we used to, but Jen is always at my side, and if I need a chat she is there in a flash; if

I need anything she's got me. Jen's now working for the Hare Krishnas in King's Cross. She refurbished the shop, made it awesome. Russell Brand had the Hare Krishnas at his book launch with Jen there serving food. She still plays her music to massive crowds and has more energy than most of my young friends. Jen is a next level magical light-warrior that blesses this planet with her existence in each moment. I must have done some things right to encounter her in this lifetime.

My Hostel in King's Cross

The day Red Jen helped me move into my hostel I sat alone on my single bed in my cold room. I felt alone, scared; wondered what this next chapter would bring.

Off a street off King's Cross, homeless drug addicts and street drinkers lined the pathway to my road: all dirty faces; smelling, but happy in the buzz of the city. A pack – a little tribe living outside KFC, opposite McDonald's. None of the other fancy cafes were there in them days: this was while King's Cross was still rough, rugged and dirty.

There was a woman – almost a skeleton – her cheeks hollow, hair patchy and thin, scraped back into a ponytail. Make-up on her face the last strand of dignity she painted onto her hollow complexion, beige to cover the volcanoes on her face from picking her skin when she got high. Businessmen from the city rode her in alleyways behind the hostel. Well, I suppose she could have had a hit to erase the pain of the encounters.

I would carry these stories with me to the building, down the stairs to the bottom floor. All the windows were fenced shut so the women couldn't come and go as they pleased. I had no key to the front door – I would ring the bell to be let through the first door that had a glass wall, which looked into the office. You'd sign your name on the board then be buzzed through to the hostel.

It felt so disgusting having staff see every entry and exit you made. There was little privacy, and the fact there were vulnerable women there was evidenced by the large number of staff. The floors were blue lino and shiny – the dirt lit up under the florescent tube lighting. The TV room where people could smoke always had a few interesting people in it. I would sit with a roll-up, chatting with the women, getting to know the way things ran around there. They shared white cider. I smoked my roll-up, knowing I didn't want to fall into that trap, 'cause I had already experienced the destruction that drink wreaks via my mum.

My first room was a box room – blood splatters on the walls welcomed me, along with sharp bins in the toilet and nasty washing areas. It was to be my home, my stable place. I felt homeless with a roof over my head. All the women were different, from diverse backgrounds. There were no cooking facilities in our rooms – most women's bodies here didn't run on food, anyway.

I heard stories for some of the women, even though we never spoke. There was one – I think her name was Catherine. She was big – not massive – but a round big, a big that suits a woman. Her long grey hair flowed over her flowing black dress tops and long skirts, crystals and brooches on her clothes. She must have been, like, 45. I saw her as a witch, a wicker woman. In hindsight I realise she must have been a woman lost in mental health problems, but in them days, with the dirty floors and walls around me, my mind made her into a more unusual character. I imagined her room had broomsticks, Ouija boards, maybe a cauldron. I wanted to knock on her door one day when I was high on magic mushrooms, but when I had come down I didn't want to open the door to a friendship.

My next door neighbour was Jamaican. We got on for the first few days I was there, then didn't, because I weren't gonna be part of the cider massive or the collective dole cheque: my dole was for getting to college. Her room was like a corridor it was so small, with a little window. I guessed she had been to prison 'cause she was so cosy in that tiny space. She was addicted to crack and had lost her son. When she was high and depressed she would shout, 'Fucking white bitch' for hours. I didn't get scared, 'cause there was a wall between us.

I had a few friends. One woman downstairs, Cheryl, was a lovely older woman, around 58 years old: not too hard on the booze; telly was a comforter for her. She was the mum of the hostel. You could go to her room and chill out, smoke a rollie, have a little drink. We caught jokes in that room; a little family was forming.

Our little sister in the group, Lacey, was a Scottish woman under 5 foot. She self-harmed 'til her arms were mutilated and she had a chronic drug addiction. We were chilling in Cheryl's room one evening and Lacey was in a bad way. She had been raped the night before. Lacey and a couple of the girls ran a con, getting the guy to a dark spot and running off with the dough. She was unlucky that night: the guy made sure he got the product first advertised. Her pain was immense, saturating the room from her pores. I liked her: a feisty woman fighting the wrong battle.

Debbie was a crack addict, also into the brown and drink. She was a mixed raced woman, curly hair tied back, quite attractive. She was loud and bubbly but I only saw her on her up days. She also sold her body and walked up York Way, asking for pounds from passers-by. She died while we were there – run over. When I heard, I had a vision of an angel being freed from beneath the car. I knew she had had enough. No more walking up York Way, begging away her life force.

Sarah lived above me – a black woman with gold teeth. I liked her a lot. She had three children that she didn't look after any more. It was sad to hear that familiar story in the hostel. Her vibrant energy shone through her addictions. She was real – not a liar or two-faced. Her motherly nature made her friends in the hostel. I wished more for her than she wished for herself. She tried to hold on to reality, but kept losing her grip. Crack stole parts of her soul, but she couldn't feel her children any more out there, away from her, so perhaps it was a comfort.

Amy – the other lesbian there – was a large woman. She was cheery and friendly, another one of the genuine crew in the snake's pit. She was always clean and well presented, made an effort. It was crack that captured her too. Amy would help me learn lines for my shows, especially when I played the shoemaker's wife in one. Sarah and Amy came to one of my shows at my college when I was studying Community Theatre. I could see them, front row, special brew in black bags, sipping during the performance. My mum didn't come: this was my genuine family, for now.

My ex Sexy P deserves her own section: she got me through that time, sexy naughty girls playing in the night. Gosh I have always found places to have fun, sexually.

If I'd chosen to take the course, this place was a university of street life. I chose college, thankfully, and enjoyed the drama of theatre, an escape from the drama in the building where I lay my head down. Not quite a home, a place to move through a stop-gap. Yet when it is all you have, it becomes your world.

Sexy P

I met her in the smoking room of my hostel: we were sat on plastic waiting-room chairs covered in burn holes, looking out the window, which was covered with a metal square grid just in case anyone tried to jump out the window. All guests had to come in one door, be seen through the glass panel then let into the hostel. She was sat there smoking her roll-up, her big lips holding the cigarette lusciously as she puffed. I was smoking my roll-up. I moved to sit next to her. She let me know within the first few words that she had been to gay clubs to pick up girls. I felt like she was telling me about myself and my actions. I thought she was part of a secret plot of people that had a crew watching me: how did she know that I went to clubs and picked up girls?

She invited me to her room. It was a small room at the top of the hostel. She told me her name was Penny aka Sexy P. We talked for a while. She was of Nigerian heritage: her African name was Nadu and she was beautiful. My heart fluttered in wonder at this young woman – intrigued but a little too naïve to know if she was flirting.

Back in my room, a floor below her, I absorbed all she said to me. She had a boyfriend, and so did I. My guy was so lovely: he would wait for me, take me on dates, introduced me to his family. He was good-looking, with gorgeous black hair, deep blue eyes, pale skin. He wore a leather jacket. I liked to fuck him, me on top; didn't like to touch his dick much, even though he had a nice one. I liked to cum, then I had no real interest; didn't care if he was still hard.

I would bump into Sexy P in the corridors, or in the canteen for dinner; the coldness of the hostel warmed up by the electricity that flowed through my body every time I saw her.

One day we were sitting in a room where the paint – a strange blue colour that reflected the mood in the room – was cracking and falling off the walls. The women were talking about who had their giro and who was buying the drinks that day. One of the women came in with blood dripping down her arms; she had been self-harming.

Penny and myself were the youngest there. The women in the hostel were living at rock bottom: homeless, drug addicts and sex workers. I looked at Penny across the table as we ate what could barely be called food. Her eyes twinkled; I wanted to know more. I watched her lips as she spoke, how her tongue moved in her mouth. I wanted to kiss her, to feel her tongue in my mouth. I got a tingle as the thoughts ran through my mind.

We were snapped back to reality by one of the crack addicts shouting at the top of her lungs about some injustice she was feeling, holding a can of strong lager in a brown paper bag. I blinked. Was this really my reality right now? When my eyes opened, I was confronted with the same scene.

Thinking of Penny gave this space meaning. I wrote poems,

went to college and thought of her. She knocked on my door one Friday night. I had a bottle of gin that a boy bought me as a gift on my desk, so I offered her a drink. We drank together and played some tunes off my little stereo that you had to balance a certain way to make work. She took off most of her clothes and danced for me. She was Sexy P: sexy like a snake. She had colourful beads around her waist. Her body moved: I was enchanted, yet felt like a rabbit caught in the headlights. I wanted to touch, to kiss, to feel her – but I'd never encountered a woman like her before, she was beyond all my experiences to date.

After she left, I went to check on her: she was naked on her bed with a pile of vomit on her carpet. I mopped up her sick, put her clothes on her, then tucked her in for the night. I wanted her, but not like that.

*****

We pushed and pulled; we played yet never touched. Eventually, we planned a night out to the Scala, a night club in King's Cross, which was proper close to where we lived. It was an urban gay event and we were on it. We got drunk up before we left, necked half a bottle of vodka. The club was dark, boyish girls stood by the walls with baggy jeans, shirts and stand-offish glares. I was feeling the tunes and getting my groove on. Penny was watching me from the side, observing my every move.

One girl in the rave waved mistletoe over my head; I leaned in for a peck on the lips. Penny shot a look at me, and I got, then, that she was interested. We dirty danced, we moved our faces close, yet didn't kiss. I was aching for her to touch me. The night felt like it was going in slow motion; I felt her every move.

Back at the hostel: we were drunk, we kissed; it was sexy, I was turned on. She got out a lacy dress from her wardrobe, threw it to me and asked me to put it on and to dance for her. We had sex. I had not had sex like this with a woman before and no man had ever made me feel this way. I left early in the morning for my job on the market stall in Camden Town. As I walked I could still feel her as if she was penetrating me in that moment.

The next night I went back to her room. She did anything but kiss me. She pulled out all her old school reports, told me about her upbringing. I was thinking, did we have the same night, the night before? Her actions were not of someone who I had lay naked with the previous night. I had been excited to see her all day, to continue the story we had started. I was so confused. She pulled out more sexy outfits. I wanted to kiss yet I didn't understand the space we were in. I had another shift the next day so I got up to leave.

She pulled me back and said she knew 'I wanted to play with her but I was not brave enough to ask.' She pulled me into her bed. We kissed. It was every moment I had wanted: I felt like I was home. She reached towards my knickers and touched me. I was too sore to go any further. She turned and said, 'I have never done that with a girl before, you talked me into it.'

Shocked and hurt, I left her room and went to mine for the night, ego bruised, heart hurt. I slept, hugging myself for warmth.

*****

It became a dance: we saw each other or we didn't. Because everyone had to sign in and out of the hostel before being let in the second door, I would know if she was in. I was scared, most of the time. With a boy, I wouldn't give a fuck; with her everything was different.

Sometimes I chilled with one of the old ladies downstairs, who had a small room with a single bed, wardrobe and not much room beyond that: few of the women in the hostel hung out there. Sharing a bottle of cider one day, I slurped down a glass. Sexy P knocked on the door, looking for tobacco. We drank a little, then went for a walk outside. It was snowing.

We jumped the fence, ran through the park, grabbing snow into balls. We had a snow fight, which led to a real fight: we grabbed each other, rolled across the snow. It was so fucking sexy. I bit her, she screamed. 'Nuff of the men from the hotels that surrounded the park came out to see what was going on. They were feeling two girls rolling about in the snow.

When we got back to her room we fucked all night, she felt how sex looks in the movies. Her skin was delicious; I ate her, licked her skin, kissed her all over. I wanted to feel every cell of who she was. We slept in her single bed, wrapped around each other – her dark skin, my pale skin. We merged in the moment of love.

We played sex games: I carved holes in the board of my bed for handcuffs; she had a whole wardrobe of sexy outfits she liked me to wear. She was clinical with sex at times: she washed her hands before touching me. Ironically I felt kinda dirty at times with her, like I was her little sex toy.

We played games with each other over staying the night: if she didn't stay with me the last time we fucked, I would go back to my room the next time we got it on, deliberately not spending the night together.

We would get drunk and get high on skunk, run through the corridors of the hostel. We got twisted one time on magic mushrooms: I wanted to eat her while high. She thought aliens were invading her body though, so that weren't on the table. The corridors looked massive to me, a space that usually felt like the walls were closing in was suddenly expansive. The mushrooms shifted my spatial awareness; this place that had once felt prison-like now looked and felt so different. She ducked out that night to see her boyfriend. I stayed alone, high in my room. We had a funny way of communicating.

I left my boyfriend; he was falling in love with me, and I was falling in love with her. I now understood what all the fuss about sex was. I think I was just missing the point when I was fucking boys. Now it all made sense. She was everything to me. One night, while we were having sex, she screamed out, 'Tell me how you feel about me.' I told her, 'I love you'. We groaned with love. I had slept with other women when drunk, but this was my first time falling in love: this time I felt something shift in my heart. I was opening up to love.

It felt strange sometimes, like when she would ask me to sit on a chair with no pants on so she could part my legs and stare at me. Some of the foreplay I had a feeling had been done to her as a child by an adult close to her. She had been sexually abused by someone close. She had never recovered from the abuse: a part of her was missing, the pain overflowed into her reality.

I loved her the best I could with what I knew of love, which weren't much. She loved me the best she could back. She took me to her family parties, big African parties. We would lock the door in the bathroom to fuck, then she would smile while the guys would try to chat me up. My sexy P, the sexy snake. We went to art shows. She came to my first ever poetry gig. I had written her poems but never read them to her – didn't wanna gas her up or give her a big head. That is something I proper regret now, because she deserved every one of those words of love.

She brought me to a strip club in Shoreditch – one of the most gross clubs, corny and cheesy – with young girls in the outfits she got me to wear, a stage near the back with a pole. The girls gyrated on the floor with a neon light that illuminated the pussy, the guys watched, drooling. The girl on the stage couldn't have been more than 18, Eastern-European looking. She went around the room with a cup to put pounds in. Sexy P grinded up on me. She was never affectionate in public. I was kinda drunk, 21 years old, long blonde hair, kinda pretty; not used to this environment. I got introduced to the boss, who kept filling up our drinks. It was the one time she was on me and I didn't want her there. He offered me some work. I kindly declined and couldn't wait to get home. We fucked that night; a drunken collision. The staff knocked on the door in the morning. I hid in the wardrobe as they did room checks. Fuck that hostel life.

*****

Sexy P left to get a semi-permanent place in East London. I missed her like crazy, and I started to be serious about getting the fuck out of there, away from the crack and smackheads and the horrors of King's Cross with the homeless lining the streets like bin bags on the corners waiting to be taken to the tip.

We kept in touch for a while; we were intimate a few more times. Then she faded out. She pursued acting, going on to do the same course I had done the year before. I heard she had left early to have a baby with the man she was seeing during our time together. Then she disappeared completely out of my life. Until one day, after like 5 years without hearing a word from her, I was in the studio – must have been 2007 – and she called me.

'Hey, baby, it's Sexy P. Remember me?'

She said she needed a mentor, like I had had. I offered to get her involved in a film that I was doing, but she said she couldn't do it 'cause she was banged up.

'Banged up?'

'Yeah baby, they locked me up in the hospital.'

She had lost it all. She had had the baby, she had had the man. But she had gone crazy because of being fucked and abused as a child.

We had both been so damaged; we hadn't known how to make our love work. Maybe it was doomed from the start; or maybe it was perfect, and we were each other's angels in that caged space.

Squat Parties

My mum got hooked up with a crew of squatter ravers: Unsound System. They were responsible for the majority of the massive parties in the 90s that left a permanent mark in London history: they found derelict buildings and moved the crew in, who would live in a sectioned-off part of the building. When the parties happened, colourful backdrops lined the walls; UV painting illuminated the grey buildings. Sound Systems set up there, a family who made money from illegal parties. My role for the events would vary: I would hand out flyers for the rave on Camden Bridge at 14 years old in my grunge clothes, with long blonde hair and purple DMs, feeling like such a grown-up 'cause I was involved: a child in an adult world.

A number would be given out – a private line that would be activated at 10pm to give out the location of the party. One time, the uni my mum had attended got squatted, the old UCL, which used to be a polytechnic on Kentish Town Road, just off Prince of Wales Road. With a queue round the block, the bass thumping, it was like a light to moths: once they got close and the ravers found the party, it was ON.

I felt special, different to the others. I was only a young teenager and I was allowed to go past the sign that said CREW ONLY. The backspace weren't at all glamorous, but in my mind it was magical: old sofas that had been found thrown out, dogs with no leads and children sleeping in corners.

A guy called Scruff, a mixed race dude with short dreadlocks in a ponytail, wearing a t-shirt and jeans and steel toe-cap boots, pulled out a wrap of speed and gave all the girls a dab: he offered me some, my heart was pounding. I was only 14, had just started year ten at school and I was scared. He kept saying 'Go on!' My friend who I had come to the rave with had already dabbed it, so I licked my finger, dabbed the wrap and then licked my tongue: it was NASTY. About an hour later, I was energetic and running about with a rush through my body. I kept looking in the mirror to see if my pupils were looking bigger: I was scared my mum's friends would be able to tell I was high, and that they would tell her.

I went back into the room and another guy offered me some more: he gave me three massive dabs and then I snorted some; my first time doing a line. I didn't like it and blew it into a tissue. Twenty minutes later, I was racing: totally flying, needed to shit, the toilets all steamed up, blocked full of shit 'n' piss with the walls dripping in sweat. I needed to go so bad that I just did the business.

I was talking to everyone; making best friends with strangers; hypnotised by the beat, I danced all night long. Unity on the dance floor, a family connected to the DJ rhythms of Techno; our unified heartbeat.

My mum's boyfriend picked us up at 4am. I went home pranging out that mum would clock I'd got high. Pupils the size of saucers but she didn't notice a thing. My ears were ringing,

I could still feel the music and my heart was pounding out of my chest. I lay on the top of my bunk bed, with my sister in the other room and my friend asleep in the bottom bunk. Surrounded by posters of Keanu Reeves and River Phoenix, I couldn't sleep. I felt like a vampire. Now I had tasted grade-A drugs, I was different. I had begun my drug-taking journey.

*****

It weren't so easy to focus in school on a Monday after a big rave on the weekend. The girls in school liked the cinema and eating out; I liked drugs and illegal parties. The girls round my flats liked cider and getting banged by the boys in the flats; I liked drugs and illegal parties. I only fit in with that world of adults: everyone treated me like I was older and I liked it.

Unsound System with Berzerka Tribe then squatted the cinema in Camden, which is now an Odeon. Back then it was one massive room. The front of the cinema is where the sound system would get set up. We hung out there during the week. I probably should have been doing homework or something like that, but I was climbing through the building with my siblings, entering between the walls and through the air vents; sitting up in the old projector room, seeing piles of powders on tables.

When the weekend hit, we would help to set the party up. It would kick off on a Saturday night and go on all through Sunday. Sometimes I would run the cloakroom, which I would set up and put out signs to get people to use it. It earned me a bit of extra money. I got myself a pair of Levi's with the profits. Everyone at school had them: it was good to fit in.

I remember being high on the dance floor, now aged 15, with my brother, aged 13, in this huge party. I grabbed a boy and kissed him, we bit up each other's necks: I was covered in love bites. Mum didn't notice and the teachers at school didn't say a thing, so I weren't worried about anything.

A couple of girls were being slightly rebellious teenagers; I was hardcore raving, drinking, smoking and using drugs, dancing in a sports bra on top of the speakers, watching the revellers below. My mum's friends provided me with drugs, or I would go around asking people at the party to sell me stuff after I had earnt some money. They weren't fussed that I was a child and I even looked younger than I was.

One time in the middle of a pumping party, one of the main guys who was running it came up to me 'cause the police were kicking open the doors. He gave me a bag of 500 pills. I ran with the pills out the back stairs. I could hear the police tryna break through the doors. I ran up the concrete stairs to the kids' room where children were sleeping, and hid them in a chimney. I kept thinking later that I could have nicked ten and sold them for a tenner each. I weren't much of a thief though. The guy never asked where the drugs were. I wonder if the builders found a bag of pills when the building was renovated. People would come back to ours after the parties and drink all day on Sundays. Our mum might fuck one of the guys: she'd just shut her door in the middle of the day while we were in the house. It always used to make my stomach feel funny. She was drinking more and more often and I used to find weed under her mattress: that's how I got to have my smokes. I thought that this was the good life: drinking and chilling on Sundays before school.

The Scottish boys who ran the parties separated from Unsound System and continued on their own just as the Berzerka tribe. They put on some huge parties around London.

One summer they squatted in the old Bingo hall on Caledonian road. We went around the party with the little money we had, trying to find someone to buy drugs off. People would line the stairs, calling the names of different drugs they were selling. We bought some E and sat on the floor with the other revellers. Some woman behind me was chatting about how doing K kept her muscles good 'cause she tensed all night when she tripped out.

We were still a little prang of taking E, especially after the Leah Betts story hit the news, a young women who had died from taking ecstasy in 1995. Her story was everywhere. She had died after taking just one pill, but we still necked it. It had a dolphin on it and was blue. We had a rush of euphoric waves of love and everything felt better than it had ever felt before. Everyone looked beautiful and I felt kinda horny when high. The lights, the techno, the connections on the dance floor, dancing for hours without thinking, fully engaged in the moment... And the moment became a full night until we were outside and it was light.

In the light of day, the parties lost their magic: the floors were a mush of dirt; my trainers had turned black... People would still be around, using drugs in plain sight with the hardcore ravers; some of them still having it up on the dance floor. This was being cool: this was being alternative. I knew about being outside of the system: fuck the system 'cause it didn't do anything for us.

*****

We found our mum and younger siblings, who had woken up in the back room. The kids were lying in, eating sweets for breakfast because it's easy to ask for money off adults who are high when you're little. Groups of people were drinking cans of beer, sitting on the pavement, the music relentless: we had had enough of the rave by then, but our mum had no intention of coming home so we had to wait until she got tired of it or went to sleep somewhere. My body felt really sensitive. I was still having tingles. I just wanted to find someone to hug, 'cause the rush was wearing off. I was craving human connection.

*****

Our mum became more and more disconnected to us as time went on. If she came home from a party she would be drinking all day on a Sunday, or fucking some guy, or not coming home at all. She would lick tongues with her lovers in front of us and have loud sex. It gave my body a crazy uncomfortable sensation, my head would spin, nothing to hold onto; the house felt like a ship on a stormy sea with no sign of land in sight.

At parties, Mum would ask people for a line, saying she had four kids and needed to stay awake. People would give her drugs, as if they were helping a single mum with powdered poison. We weren't really close enough for me to let her know I was using grade-As. She knew I smoked and by 15 years old I was smoking cannabis on a daily basis, supplied by my mum's mates. The guys who ran the parties all got hooked on serious drugs; the main crew became smack and crack-heads, with a good few turning to the drink real bad. We watched people who came to London with dreams of beating the system, who went from earning good money running parties to sleeping rough, begging for enough change for drugs.

This all felt so normal for a time, until Mum stopped coming home from the parties and we would be calling everyone, trying to find her. By year11, just barely 16 years old, I was partying more and using more drugs. Home life was becoming unbearable. I felt like an outsider: I didn't fit in at home or on the estate. Once I had felt cool, but now all I felt was alone.

March for the Alternative

12.20pm. I waited with Sonority, my wonderful friend I had met through the poetry scene, on the Blackfriars Bridge, while floods of people filled up the streets, the atmosphere alive with unity and a wanting to be heard. Samba bands rhythmically moved the crowd, dancing surrounded the beats, raising the energy as they started on their journey for the day. The elderly in wheelchairs were pushed along, holding slogans: 'Where's my pension?' These are the people who represented us at war, now cut out by a government representing the rich. Youth workers, teachers, nurses, marching, banners held high, colourful clothing; a mass sea of melted colours, marching against cuts to our services, objecting to our services being stolen from the poor.

We waited, absorbing the energy, keeping it safe in our souls to share on the mic as soon as the sound system arrived. Bikes moulded together with the infrastructure of a rainbow dragon went past, blaring music with a tribe of dancers entranced in the breaks. Tidal waves of protesters passed us. Massive speakers, blaring basslines, the vibrations flowing through the embankment. While we set up, we attracted a bunch of ravers – crusty types, beer in hand, dirty clothes, piercings and a dreadlock-style of hair. The crusties reminded me of pirates, travelling through London wearing random clothes and with spirits that roamed free.

We finally got mobile, brought the sound system into the march; Andy riding the bike up front with 'the only good system is a sound system' written on his back. We jam-packed the roads usually reserved for cars and traffic, roads filled up with passion, marching to make a stand. We plugged in the system's loud music and took to the mic, walking ahead of the system so as to not cause feedback. A call and response to the people: 'I say "no", you say "cut-backs"… No… Cut-backs.' Such a unified atmosphere, all together for the same cause, supporting each other: the street felt like home. Sonority, Ed Frees – a revolutionary rapper – and I led our section of the march with positive, conscious messages, Ed getting the crowd to chant: 'Come on feds: join our side it's more fun,' hoping they would hear our invite.

We passed a bride and let out cheers as if we were all one voice, the acoustics emphasizing the sound. We called: 'Make some noise for unity!' The crowd cheered, all around whistles and horns were blowing. Smiles from hearts released into the London vibe. We bumped into friends and beautiful girls and boys showed appreciation for the energy and lyrics we were sharing.

When we realised we were at the back of the march, we wheeled the system up the road on the pavement and got back into the thick of the crowd. Conscious hip-hop played through the demo. A bunch of older Caribbean women were following us, dancing to the beats and lyrics of Lowkey, Logic and many other UK rappers speaking the truth. A group in front of us, dressed in suits, five of them – men and women – held chains around the neck of a guy in the middle, who was wearing a David Cameron mask. He had fake blood on his costume and the other actors held clubs and batons and pretended to hit him. Boos as we passed Downing Street: different cultures, different ages, all feeling the same emotion. A young girl held up a sign that read, 'R.I.P. education'. I bumped into Jessica, an old friend from back in the day, taking photos and running ahead to capture the scene. There was a guy on top of one of the statues as we started to approach Trafalgar Square: rebellion alive, with brave warriors wanting their disgust at the cuts to be noticed and noted.

We arrived at Trafalgar Square and set up the system again, this time behind the lions facing the roundabout. Sonority, Kai and I had some food – I had some oatcakes with hummus, very hippy of me. I forgot my carrot sticks. I got a bottle of pink cava: the vibes, the bubbles always livened up my spirit. Rob the Rub sat up by the lions, guitar in hand, the mic-stand reaching him. He played a set to the crowd on the pavement, a funny, conscious, acoustic set. Abandoned homemade placards lay on the ground: 'Tax the banks 0.00.5% per transaction, raise 25 million pounds globally PA… Robin Hood tax'.

We noticed the crowd was drying up and decided to get a move on to Hyde Park through the roads with the music blaring. From Trafalgar we headed towards Piccadilly Circus, 15 of us skipping forward, my bottle of cava in hand perfectly matching my outfit; the pink drink and my bright pink laces with purple jacket made quite an impression on these streets. Marching forward we resurrected the rally, just as people were losing the vibe for the day. We became pied pipers of the rally. A bigger crowd joined us as we moved forward; people walking towards us joined us, going back the way they had come from. On Regent Street, in the middle of the road, I got on the mic, getting the crowd to cheer. They went crazy loud, cheers filled the streets: the consumers on the pavement look confused. We did some more call and response: 'When I say "freedom", you say "fighters" ... Freedom ... Fighters'. Such a powerful feeling. I followed the crowd's energy and freestyled to the beats, with photographers running in front, taking pictures of our demonstration.

We reached Oxford Circus, where a fire in the middle of the junction acted as a physical symbol of the flames of anger burning inside the people. I felt the moment and rapped from my soul, bless the mic: 'You can knock us down and give us cuts, but we'll find a way through and just get back up.' Then, 'Make noise for freedom!' The crowd was with us, supporting the messages over the beats through the mic: such power through a unified response.

As we set off down Oxford Street, shoppers watched us from the sidewalk as if we were animals from the zoo. We now had around 150 followers joining us through the commercial capital. Ed Frees chanted, 'Down with the government, down!' The crowd sang along with cheers and determination. We had the raving crews with us. Years of living in the bubbles of parties creates rebellious spirits.

Booming drum 'n' bass as we reached Marble Arch and the corner of Hyde Park. The traffic had started to make its way through but was stopped by our procession. We skipped through the concrete. I said, 'Who wants to party???' More cheers. The mic work was becoming a real job, keeping spirits high and violence to a minimum.

Outside Hyde Park, more fires blazed, and we got another couple of hundred protesters to follow us. Clapper Priest was there, which was great, as he vibed up the mic: new energy got the crowd really bouncing, with strong positive energy released into the atmosphere. We turned back towards Oxford Street, a few hundred following us. The vibes were live. Another MC joined us and was in with the conscious lyrics, keeping the vibe friendly.

As we marched forward I saw a few of my friends: O.P. and Sarai were there – warrior sisters. They joined our procession. I was speaking lyrics of unity, of peace, of the power of our vibrations as we danced and cheered through the West End. We turned down Regents Street, at least 500 followers when I looked back: I couldn't see the end of the people in the groove

We almost reached Piccadilly, dodged our way through a mass park-up of meat wagons. Through the side street we saw riot police running, looking to circle and kettle us; we turned back and moved back through Regent Street, still vibing the mic... Ed and I shared perfectly. It was taking serious amounts of energy to move the crowd and keep it peaceful.

Down Oxford Street, down Wardour Street, through Soho we went; the acoustics of a smaller street made the mic all the more powerful. Ed went off with the mic, leaving responsibility with me. I kept the crowd bouncing and moving with great vibrations. It was so fun and exciting, running past police and owning the roads that belonged to us anyway! Reclaiming the land from the cars and shops.

Down Wardour Street, we collected more People Power as we travelled, down the back alleys right through to Trafalgar Square. We set up by the lions in the centre of the square again. I climbed up by the lion, with the mic: we now had 2,000 people surrounding us, the crowds dancing out to the beats, with a fire roaring.

I shared lyrics of unity, poetry flowing in freestyle; rhyme from a higher source. I channelled the messages. I felt the energy of the crowd and how easily a happy party could turn into a riot.… Standing by the lion, I felt how strong we could be as a unit, how we could change this world with love, with peace and conscious thoughts and actions. I shared more lyrics with the crowd: they cheered, responded to call and response in the most inspirationally beautiful way!

It was like glitter was leaving my mouth, going through the system and out through the speakers – glittering our ravers with light, love and sparkles! We were the non-violent segment of the parade. Davis – a rapper I met that day – shared the mic with me, which I welcomed: I'd used every drop of my energy. The crowd shouted and chanted love, together unified, dancing as we remembered that this world is owned by no man or woman. Another MC crew arrived with positive energy so I retired from the mic, amazed at our spontaneous march and the power of the people.

Fireworks went off, lighting the sky with pretty splashes of silver. Flares went off and there was a couple of other sound systems entertaining people, and singers with guitars talking of freedom.

I danced with the crew in the crowd before going off to get some wine. I stood on some steps just outside Trafalgar Square. Davis, the other MC, joined me: we shared wine, no glasses, watching as police van after police van surrounded the area – shields, helmets and batons out, they ran forward as a massive gang to break up the peaceful party. Anger stung the air and sparked the crowd to fight back.

Glad to be free of that, I marched with our sound system for a short while, and then decided to get the bus home, my energy stretched for the day, but full of optimism from the energy we'd created. I knew that riots had kicked off and a lot of the media would choose to show that. My experience was full of love and unity, the strongest I had ever felt it! I know we can make real change to this world. Keep fighting with a pure heart and anything is possible!

Gay

My mum sat us round the table in the kitchen, her four children (she had us all within six years). I was about 12, my bro 10, my younger brother 8 and my sister 6 years old. In our bright yellow kitchen, bright like our mother's heart when she still felt the sunshine. It was one of them family talks, where she needed to address us all at once. We would sit quietly, waiting for what was to come.

I didn't want to be there, my mind was wandering, eyes looking at the old pieces of our art on the walls as the ripped corners of them danced in the breeze.

'I know one of ye is going to be gay'

What!? How could she be saying this right now?

'A mother knows her children and I have four of ye, so one of ye is going to be gay.'

I was thinking, Oh shit it's me, it's me, it's me: I hope no-one can tell that it's me. Fuck, can she see in my eyes what I'm trying not to say? It felt like my thoughts were being blasted through a megaphone; my heart beat like a djembe.

This is one of my clearest first memories of being confronted with the possibility of having to come out, to acknowledge my sexuality and all that I didn't want to be. The moment passed, but I thought, Is this really my life?…. I'm broke; my dad has gone, left us; he is addicted to Heroin; my mum's hitting the drink real hard, and our family are a joke on this estate. FUCK BEING GAY!! FUCK U LIFE ON A REALNESS!!

*****

Our estate: so grey we never saw rainbows, even after it rained and the sun shone. No one was out 'n' proud. It was tracksuits without any exercise (unless ur running 'cause ur being chased by the feds); big gold earrings that scraped the shoulders; harsh voices.

I didn't get on with the girls round my area: I didn't like them. I didn't wanna fuck boys at the back of the basketball pitch then drink cider till I passed out. I wore my Nirvana t-shirt and purple DMs. I was already a target. They moved in a pack; I was a lone wolf. They hunted me, shouting across the bricks, bouncing off the blocks, 'SHAUNA YOU LESBIAN'.

That cut deep, as I knew it was the truth…. Home was a war zone, the flats a maze and I had yet to find the exit. They had my Achilles heel.

I felt so isolated; all I wanted to do was kiss a woman. I would have crushes at school, heart beating like crazy for certain girls; watching, wishing I could ask them out, but boys were the safer option. I wanted to fit in somewhere.

Feeling like a square peg in a society where you need to fit into the round hole: that was my school, my home, my estate; thinking that survival was more important than expressing who I knew I really was.

I lost my virginity to a boy. It was shit – on a floor in some room with my mate, while she fucked some other boy. My mum said she would know when I lost my virginity, but when I come home with my friend, I looked in the mirror in my mum's room and she couldn't tell; probably 'cause she had been drunk the night before.

I had a couple of boyfriends. I thought I loved them but I always wanted to know what it was like with a woman.

One day I just thought: I need to know, I need to kiss a girl. I went down the road from my place in Tottenham to a phone box. I called a gay and lesbian helpline. The guy on the phone told me about the Candy Bar in Soho an all-girl club. I decided to go that night, alone. I got myself drunk up before I went. I got in – I didn't know anyone. I saw so many different women, all colours, sizes, different styles. I guess I was drunk enough now to chat to a girl. I let the her know I had never kissed a girl before, that this was brand new to me. She kissed me. I closed my eyes. Her lips were so soft, so succulent, so delicious. We kissed for hours, then I left to walk through the West End with her and her mates. I invited her back to mine: she said no, but gave me her number on a piece of paper. I lost her number on the way home when I stopped in a phone box to roll a joint to smoke before I went back. I proper regretted that joint for a while.

It became a routine for a bit: I would go out, get drunk, find women and have sex with them. I didn't much know what I was doing. I would try my best to be good at it, but tryna ya best don't make ya amazing. Then home life got all messed up again, so I forgot about finding myself through my sexuality for a little while anyway.

Then there was him and him and him. The last one really was loving, sweet, devoted, introducing me to his family at Christmas, waiting for me outside of my hostel in King's Cross, walking me home, buying me flowers. Sex felt OK: I could come if I grinded on him. The rest was alright... He was there, I was just about... Then I met her.... Sexy P

The soft feeling of our bodies together, dancing naked in love, finally making me feel 'normal'. How had it taken me so long to explore this? Why did I have so much guilt leading up to this moment?

My moments with her were beautiful; our kisses colourful like a garden of the finest flowers; a sweet smell; an aroma that aroused the soul. The teenage cuss words, 'gay', 'lesbian', made no sense in that space. Making love tangled in emotions, our tongues spoke the body's language: it was bliss.

She was seen as my 'friend' at family gatherings, even though I made it clear she was my girlfriend. My dad always asked after my brother's girlfriend but never asked about her. When Hollyoaks came on at home, Dad would turn it off, 'cause there was a gay storyline, which he thought was brainwashing. His theory was that, if you were caught young, 'they' could get you and your brain would be corrupted. This was his understanding of homosexuality. He told me he was nearly converted by a gay when he was younger, that it was lucky he made it past that man and is straight.

I was afraid to stand up for myself about the way I felt love, 'cause I was afraid of being shut down. I didn't even respect my dad after watching him shoot heroin and smoke crack. Yet

I cowered and tried to be 'normal'.

People seemed to act so liberal about homosexuality, but then I stepped back and really listened to their opinions. I would like to say I'm totally 'out 'n' proud', yet there are times I still struggle to share this aspect of myself with people. I worked in a youth club, where the opinion was shared that being gay was a choice. I would sit in the meetings and hear these opinions that were presented as facts. I'd say that I didn't choose to be gay; that I wanted anything but this tag attached to my life. It was just that once my heart felt the heart of a woman, my whole life made sense.

I think of the countries where it is illegal to be gay, where people get stoned for the way they feel LOVE! The world's projection of what is right and what is wrong makes no sense to the rhythm of my heartbeat, to the heartbeats of those of us who stand up to say we are proud of how we experience LOVE. Being in love with a woman is one of the most beautiful experiences in my life: I have no need to apologise for all that I am. United, we make the stand!

Loving Deeper

the love falls through the cracks of insecurities;
open hearts beat through chests, exposed, naked.
two females, contours, shapes, moans, groans of ecstasy...
not an egotistic connection, but a soulful dance, expressed outside
of the human form.
souls intertwine in divinity. rhythm, hot beats, sometimes tears as this
intensity was unexpected.
we lie together, one hot from giving, the other relaxed from an earth-
shattering orgasm.
body on body, face by face, eyes together, tears mixing as a reminder
of the oneness of the universe. speechless! what good is a word
when the body is speaking through a megaphone?
after many breaths, sobs, a hug so close, as if we may never get a
moment like this again, the breaths pass, the souls return from the
dance, and we are once again naked, vulnerable, exposed to a deeper
love.
the speech returns and
she asks, 'why are you crying?'
i chicken the chat and say, 'why are you crying?
she speaks of feelings as if it were easy. in the throws of sex i throw
my emotions to the wind. our molecules... the molecular speaks
louder than the scaredy cat i become.

the tears don't lie, as she verbalises, the stains on my face and red eyes speak all the words i'm unable to say.

no script to this scene, the emotions are improvising, creators of our reality as all there is is this moment.

as we travel deeper into the realm of becoming partners, the physical expressions unburden all the wrongdoings, and sayings.

no lies exist as love is made, the heart trying to be unsaid speaks volumes. us, we only, brand new together have already hurt one another. yet the pain gives more room for our love.

kisses erase the unintentional moves outside of one's true self.

when we make love we really feel love! we return to who we really are without the distractions we create in our own minds.

our true essence, all we are is love. a reminder of our true form.

love conquers all.

Reebok Classics

I remember trying to fit in, rocking Reebok Classics. Mine were vintage: totally in an unfashionable way, 'cause on the estate it was all shiny new sportswear and big gold chains. My classic reeboks were a pale mustard colour with dark blue stripes, beyond dirty, with rips along the side and worn down on the bottom without any grip. I had to put them on every day and try and walk with dignity through the estate; every day hoping not to bump into a peer 'cause I didn't have any friends and didn't fit in.

Every day was stressful, leaving the flat, wondering if I could make it to Camden High Road without getting hassle. My trousers were from Kookai yet had a hole in the bum, a rip. I wore a jumper around my waist to hide the hole. I had around five t-shirts, one old dirty jacket, nasty underwear… It was an embarrassment to be me.

We never had much, with Mum scrounging by, all her money going on drink. We suffered in a place full of suffering. I had ducked out of school before my exams as I couldn't make sense of this world, and the brick maze I found myself trapped in was suffocating me. I tried to imagine myself as an actress: I would daydream about being discovered on the street 'cause the TV sold miracle stories, which made fame look easy. In reality I would wake and roll a joint, put on the same clothes as yesterday, the same shoes I had been wearing for a year, look out my window to the grass below with someone walking a dog looking miserable. I would really try to dream of a way out, then walk in the living room and see my mum and her friends drunk. I would drink too, and the soft fuzzy haze made the nightmare bearable for a few hours. My heart would burn from helplessness every morning and the fights with Mum became increasingly violent and vicious. I didn't know what self-image was or what it meant; I had no identity: I tried to fit into the hippy world my mum introduced me to.

So little money and zero opportunities: I had no idea how to live a life of having a job, working hard and creating a future. I grew up around drug dealers and drug abusers; everyone ducking the system, and this system was taking me down. In my hostel I lived on £33 job-seekers allowance every week. My hostel rent was £16 a week and it was £7 a week for my bus pass, leaving me with £11 to live off. The hostel made a meal every day for the residents as part of the deal of living there. I was at college most days but had to get the food as I had no money to cook an alternative. I still didn't have many clothes and did my best not to graduate to the college of prostitution or selling drugs. Those ways to hustle lead to despair.

I watched my friends with their nice phones: BlackBerrys on contract, they could make a call whenever they wanted to and had loads of texts. I was tryna arrange gigs, and could only call people on the weekend when I had 60 minutes and free texts. If I missed a call I would text with my credit, hoping they would call back – but usually the moment had passed by then. I wondered how to live beyond the day-to-day, but I couldn't see past the day-to-day. But I got by. I had a vision and a feeling in my heart that I could create so much more than the world I was living in; if I only knew how to create it.

The Good Side of My Mum

My mum's many sides were not all dark, amongst the destruction there was also light. My beautiful mum, with her bright orange hair, piercing blue eyes and freckled skin; always talkative, a real storyteller. Her naivety became my wisdom, attracting so many different souls into our lives. Different shoes she wore over the years painted a colourful existence.

She played with, and encouraged our imaginations consistently. As a child I would sit and talk to angels in my room: instead of telling me I was stupid or that there was no such thing, she would ask what we spoke about.

Food was a ritual; we always ate around the table: four children, our mother and whichever of her boyfriends was living with us. At the table, we learnt Irish history, all about the Vikings' tales our mother had learned as a child. We would talk about our dreams; our mother knew the importance the dream world had on our lives.

When we were young, from birth till around my tenth year, Mum was a Christian. Church was every Sunday. I loved

Church. I had an amazing relationship with God. I would get kids to pray with me in the playground at infant school. At like seven years old I would frequently speak in tongues. Mum had grown up as a strict Catholic in Ireland. She didn't want us to grow up Catholic, but still made sure God was part of our lives. Our house was filled top to bottom with books. She read every single one of them. As a child I'd see Shakespeare, Plato, Virginia Woolf lining our shelves. I would see her in the morning in bed with a big thick book; by lunch-time she was half way through; by the end of the day she would have finished it. I thought she had magic powers, being able to read so fast.

We would create tents in our rooms with sheets; we would travel to Australia, space and lands not yet discovered, all under the cushions in the living room. Not everyone on the estate was allowed such creative freedom.

Her singing voice was so beautifully enchanting. When she left Christianity she went back to university as a mature student to study English Literature. At her uni – well, it was the north London polytechnic on Prince of Wales Road in Kentish town back then – she made lots of friends. Our house was full to the brim with students of all different ages playing instruments and smoking joints. She learnt to play the guitar. We had a few favourite songs she would play and we'd harmonise, our melodies intertwining; sounds skipping around the orange walls of our kitchen. When there were visitors, I would know that if I heard the guitar move and 'SHAUNA!' shouted loud, it was time to sing to our visitors. Singing together was our sacred land, our truce. She was an incredible writer, with impeccable english skills; her stories touched souls.

Our holidays were always magical: our mum would take us to

Ireland; off to the family, or to see friends in one of our favourite locations like the Brecon Beacons in Wales. Getting away to the Beacons was a welcome escape from the tower blocks and constant police sirens; a green paradise, free from the concrete jungle. We would get a packed lunch and go walking all day in the mountains. We felt like warriors, connecting with the wisdom of the soil in those hills. That freedom our mother provided was invaluable; children running with nature, embracing Mother Earth.

Skin to skin contact was a norm; four children in a bath together, naked as we were born. We bathed with our mum, girls and boys together. I still love to share baths to this day; it's ingrained in my being. After the bath, we would run around the house singing naked. All children love being naked: to accept your body at such a young age is a real gift; loving your shape.

We learned the art of a healing touch from youth: Mum was renowned for her massages; the living room a chilled vortex in those moments. I would massage my mum and her friends. I could earn a fiver for the cinema if I gave my mum's friends a full body massage, some cool hippy women.
There were always so many different people staying at our flat. We were constantly influenced by the intelligent conversations and musical instruments around us.

I keep those good moments where my mum's light shone bright, with me always.

Koh Phangan

I made a plan to leave London for Thailand for the winter. Christmas always brings rough depression as a gift; a reminder of my mother losing her fight, and that our family weren't like the ones you see in Christmas films. I was determined that this year would be different; this year I would go to Paradise. I would spend Christmas Day on a beach and I would be happy. I had one stable job that covered my rent, a couple of jobs here and there that covered my food and clothes, then a couple of freelance creative projects that brought in the extra cash. I had £1,800 saved to get out of town and visit Asia. My good friend Belle had told me of a magical community on the island of Koh Phangan, at a resort called The Sanctuary. She was the second person to mention it to me after my friend Francesca. I went for a coffee with another good friend, Danni, we were connecting over some ideas for music projects, Danni ran a pionering event called OneTaste in London for many years which attracted incredible cliental, and she also recommended the place, saying she would be there over Christmas. The universe had spoken: Koh Phangan would be my destination. I let a few of my friends know that I was going, and my best friend Lena and our mutual friend, graffiti artist Pixie, joined for the adventure as well.

We left booking the holiday until super late, like a few days before we wanted to leave late. Me and my girl crew the LC Collective which comprised of Shay D, DJ Shorty and Sirena Reynolds, all people I have met through the music scene, had a gig on the night of 21st December, so it weren't the best time to be booking tickets for Thailand, not when we had a last minute rehearsal. Eventually we looked online: everything was way over the grand mark; it seemed like the whole world wanted to go to Thailand, and the extortionate fares reflected that. We called a travel company that was offering £650 fares but that was only if we left on the 26th. I weren't in the mood to be leaving after Christmas: the thought of staying was too much.

We called another dude but the web page his company had was so dodgy, Heathrow was spelt Hethrow, I didn't trust an unknown, unverified site with our card details. We decided it was better to book in the morning once we'd got the gig out the way, so we linked up the next day in Pixie's flat in Tottenham, and we chanted to the wall. We looked at flights, found more people to talk to on the phone, then a flight came up on Skyscanner: £1000 each, leaving that night and coming back on the 10th of Jan; 3 full weeks in paradise. Yes, yes! We booked it, I transferred the cash out of my account, and then went home to pack my bag for Paradise.

Although I was excited, I was scared too – I'd not left Europe before. Bag packed and within a few hours we were on the platform at King's Cross ready for an adventure. Lena's mum came to see her off, which was very sweet.

The plane was huge: I'd only flown Ryanair or EasyJet before; this was my first long haul. We zoned out to in-flight films and I chatted to a guy from the music industry sitting nearby; he worked with a well known underground rapper. We stopped off in Bahrain where we were told we had a hotel to stop over in while we waited for the connecting flight. We were given a taxi to a swish hotel. Soon as we reached our beds we crashed out. The hotel was playing Christmas music and had a tree with lights but it felt all out of sync not like at home; an alternative reality of Christmas. I had not yet experienced Christmas in another country, this was new and different, as it being an Arab country there isn't such an empathis on this holiday. I have always hated this time of year, it holds so many sad memories, I welcomed the change. We hit the buffet after our nap, glad to have food that didn't come in a little box.

We had hours to kill. Time for an adventure. We were in Bahrain: what could we do? The sky was dusty, the roads made into blocks, with sand everywhere. It seemed like an endless desert, but with skyscrapers for hotels all around.

We found a mosque and went to investigate. We were greeted with friendly faces and were rushed to a changing room to put on hijabs to respect the space. We covered our funky clothes and hair with beige cloths. We were introduced to our guide and brought into the most magnificent courtyard: it was tiled, with mosaics on the walls. The guide was very happy to be introducing us to his religion, and explained the summer practise with prayers happening in the courtyard. Then we were brought into the main hall, a gigantic room; wide, with high ceilings, decorated with art fit for a king. We were introduced to Islam. The main thing I remember he said was that God must exist, because if we humans were the cars, who was the driver? The driver is God.

Us all being Buddhists, we didn't connect to this philosophy so much. My friend Lena introduced our guide to our Buddhist beliefs, while Pixie and I went on ahead bussin' up while trying not to be disrespectful; we needed a little light relief. He was a wonderful man, he showed us the baths where you washed your feet before praying. He was very passionate about his beliefs and was doing his best to get us into his way of thinking. London girls already on a different spiritual path, he had his work cut out for him. Our belief is centred around the idea that we are all creators of our own worlds and that a transformation of the human heart creates a transformation in society. We clashed with smiles and from a respectful space and we left graciously, with joy in our hearts and an insight into to a world we hadn't seen before.

It was suddenly time to get the connecting flight. We were driven back to the airport and we were on the plane for another seven hours or so before arriving in Bangkok. The airport was beautiful, with statues made of gold, and it smelled different to London. We weren't sure of where we were going to go or where we should be. Pixie had done some research and found that the VIP coach was the best way to travel. We got a cab to the bus station, the blinding sun and heat hitting our tired sun-deprived bodies. I was in wonder and full of excitement as we shot down the highway, the cars all beeping at each other, constantly beep beep beep. There weren't the usual driving lanes that everyone stuck to like back home, and families all piled onto motorbikes without helmets, sometimes five people to a bike. Like, how do they do that, weaving in and out of the traffic, beeping with babies on their laps?!

I checked for graffiti on the highway as we sped through Bangkok in a taxi, I was afraid we would miss our bus, I was also facinated at the landscpae in this new land to me. We finally arrived at the bus station. It was a small shopping mall, we had to find our way around. It was sickly hot, we were tryna figure out the money and how much we needed for things and how much for a meal and a drink. It was 500 baht to £10 and most meals were around 100 baht, so £2 for a decent meal. We ran, tryna make the 10.30am bus but missed it and had to wait until the evening for the next bus.

With time to kill, we grabbed a tuk-tuk, which is a motor-driven rickshaw. We drove to Khao San Road to check into a hotel for a few hours to rest our bodies and shower before our next journey. Feeling refreshed, we wove through the traffic with the horn beeping, the sun pounding with the heat of the day: this was living. We were so excited. Eventually we got the bus and reached our next hotel with a little garden outside and a pool: it cost £15 for a night, so we booked a basic room with a huge double bed, a fan, and a shower. It was too hot for blankets, yet I guess we still wanted the comfort of our bodies being covered even in 28 degrees, we had a thin sheet for cover, it felt good on our tired skin. We slept for a bit during the afternoon as we had a day in Bangkok before we could get the bus out, I woke first, all hot and bothered – maybe napping in the day sharing a bed with two others was a bit much for me.

I got into the cold shower – I guess the cold water felt welcomed because it was so hot. I normally have a dread of the cold water, dunno why – probably an English thing. We're not used to the weather being as super hot and humid as it was in Bangkok – we need the warm water to get our bodies going in the cold mornings. Yet I needed the cold shower to get my body moving in that hot city.

Leaving the others to lie in, I left the hotel to go and explore the city. There were lots of tuk-tuks on the road beeping, and there were fruit and veg stalls outside every shop, fruit cut up into plastic bags, on steel wheels with glass fronts. Freshly cut fruit that looked so perfect, I got a big bag of fruit for 50p. In that moment, I was a very happy woman. I walked through an alleyway where there were lots of hotels, with tourists sitting in the bars in the shade sipping beers; people from all over the world. I felt like I was in a film. It had taken me 33 years to get out of Europe: I was so excited to be there, my heart beamed brighter than the sun.

I wandered the tight streets, past market stalls with Buddha statues and tie-dye t-shirts, all sold for a few quid. The streets were tight, no pavement it was dirt roads, I checked out the tattoo shops, measuring up the prices. Shoes have to be taken off to enter shops and cafe's which seemed strange to me as my feet where proper filthy, getting used to a new culture alone. After a while, I met up with the girls and we got a tuk-tuk back to the bus depot. We ran through the depot super-fast, as we were running late for our bus (again), and we'd already paid for it. We made it with minutes to spare.

It was a lovely bus; big seats that went back, air con, a blanket for each seat and a small packed lunch. I tried my best to sleep as it was a 12-hour journey and we were travelling through the night, my body clock in its own rhythm.

The bus stopped in the middle of the night and we were asked to get off. I was thinking, er, what about my bags...

I was totally paranoid about my bags: I wanted them close by, and not being able to communicate with the bus conductor did not help much. We were in the middle of nowhere and it was pitch black, there was some kind of cafe, and a couple of open market stalls which sold sweets, crisps and ice-cream. It was dusty and warm; dogs wandered free, in the dark it's even harder to judge what else is around, this looked like the only place to stop for miles in any direction. I noticed a three-legged dog walked past at one point. We were given a food ticket and sent into a bright hall to eat. I was given rice in a bowl of warm water. I weren't feeling it. My girls ate some of the meat, which looked like it had come from God knows where, so I ducked out of the meal and bought some crisps from a shop that was connected, I was overwhelmed with all the choice and the new flavours on offer we didn't get back home; the excitement of trying something new, even if it was just crisps.

We got back on the bus and continued our journey until the bus pulled up to Surat Thani. It was Christmas Day, 2014, 6am and we were at the edge of Paradise. The sea was turquoise and the beach looked perfect, with white sand; the rocks and cliff edges were triangle shaped. I couldn't believe we had made it there: the perfect Christmas was happening. Stray dogs ran about, and backpackers from all over were waiting for the ferries.

We grabbed some coffee and chilled for a couple of hours. On the ferry to Koh Phanngan, we found space in the ocean, no land for miles around, just focussed on the horizon. Lena got chatting to a boy, who informed us that we wouldn't be able to find anywhere to stay on the island because we had left it too late, that we would most likely be staying on the beach. This fear echoed through the mouths of others. I was just loving the sun, the light filling up my being, washing away the London grey that had been getting me down.

When we reached the island, it was baking hot, dirt roads with palms trees the sea behind us, there were trucks blaring house music with adverts on the side of them advertising parties, jungle raves, waterfall raves, full-moon parties... We found a public telephone and Lena called The Sanctuary. They had three beds in one of the dorms: we were fully blessed for our trip. Lena had lost her card, which was a pain, and my card had been blocked by my bank, even though I had let them know I was leaving the country. First world problems in the developing world feel different.

To reach The Sanctuary where we were staying, we got into a 4x4 truck, sat in the back. We went over bumpy, super high roads that wound up and up impossible hills. I was screaming for real, it was so fucking scary, like a rollercoaster without the safety belts. Children zoomed past us on motorbikes – no helmets, one sitting on the handlebars. I thought I had guts on my estate, but there on the island I felt like a baby. We reached Haad Ren. This is the town that the majority of the tourists go to have the full moon parties. We saw a sign that lead us to the taxi boat, I was thankful we didn't get taken to the jungle to be killed, I was shitting it on that taxi ride, it's funny what the mind does when you're in a new place.

We got into the taxi boat that was to bring us to The Sanctuary. On it, we met a guy who said he planned to come for a week and was still there a month later. The boat was small, an oblong shape, with a motor at the back. One man steered from the back, and another man sat with him. It jumped over the waves and we got splashed all over, but it was hot so we didn't mind. It was scary being out in the middle of the ocean, trusting people with our lives, people that we couldn't fully communicate with. It took 20 minutes to reach the beach.

When we arrived, it was everything and more than we could have asked for.

We dragged our bags over the sand, through palm trees until we reached The Sanctuary. Our London friends were there having dinner on a long table. We ran up to them and we all hugged. We were greeted by Natasha, a gorgeous woman, close to 40 in age, with a slim, beautiful body: wearing wings made out of sticks, she glided across the floor. Her magnetism was self-evident. The magic of this space was enchanting.

To get to our dorm room, we were walked through the lounge and bar, then up some winding steps. There were thick mattresses on the floor with an insect net over them. We had a little table each for our things. There were geckos in the room. It felt like being in a treehouse: on our veranda we could see out through the jungle to the sea. I never thought I could make it somewhere so awe-inspiring. I'd come from the dark days with no money to finding Paradise, where I was to live for three weeks.

Everyone we met was kind, friendly, full of love: the conversations were conscious, the food healthy and vibrant. There were so many classes to take part in. I signed up for yoga straight away. It was Lena's birthday on 28th December: we left that morning for the 10am yoga class, but on our way out one of the bars was playing music and the whole area was pumping. We heard 'Good life, good life the good life' ringing out, and we were off for a rave: yoga could wait for another time.

Guys bar was full with psychedelic dancers dressed in incredible clothes, the music pumping banging house tunes; people were barefoot under the blazing sun, fully havin' it up. This weren't a big druggie party, it was people turning up for a dance after their morning meditation practice. We met a gorgeous mixed-race girl called Sierta. She was a professional contemporary dancer. We caught vibes on the dancefloor and fully let loose. The energy was uplifting. Lena had a coconut with rum, pixie and I wasn't drinking, so we stuck to coconut water. I never dance when out in London, but now out there I was fully involved, my body moving without thought: I was in heaven.

We jammed at the beach for the rest of the day then we hit a Cacao ceremony that evening. We drunk raw cacao which is melted raw chocolate in a drink, a plant medicine that opens up the heart. We were on a platform in the jungle, with netting overhead to protect us from the insects; it was starting to get dark. We sat in a circle, around 30 of us, drinking the cacao and dancing into the night. There were two jugs of cacao, which were blessed and passed around the circle in opposite directions. We filled the cup with intentions and shared our intentions with each other. After each person shared they said 'Ahoy' which was a way of finishing sharing with the group with an acknowledgement, the group then said 'Ahoy' back. It was my turn: I was shaking. I said that I wanted to heal from my mum's death and to be able to open up, sexually and emotionally. I wanted to be able to trust people again and to heal from the pain.

We broke the circle and were allowed to hug each other but had minimal talking. Danni came up to me and gave me a massive hug. 'Shauna, you are loved,' she said. The tears flowed from all the cracks in my heart, pouring all over Danni and all over me, down our arms. I felt the pain rise, I wanted to push her away, to say that this pain is mine and no one must ever feel it with me. She pulled me closer and we both wept. We let go, then we started to dance led by Daisy who was holding the space for the evening. We danced in the elements: fire, wind, water, air and earth; an ecstatic dance, twirling, making shapes, rolling across the floor. Then I settled into a meditation, cross-legged on the floor. I connected to my mum's spirit and apologised for all the pain and hurt we caused each other. I cut Karmic cords and sobed some more, a waterfall. An ache passed through my eyes and now it was I who wore the tears like diamonds, glistening: they were indestructible like my spirit; I glistened with pride.

I saw a beautiful young woman dressed all in red, rolling on her back, with her legs and arms in the air, like a graceful beetle. I had to know her. When the ceremony ended, we spoke and hit the cafe for a vegan cake to see the evening off to a perfect ending. She's Scottish and carried herself like a queen, her soft accent a lullaby and we were in a dream together on that perfect night. An instant connection, we became best friends on the island, and she joined our crew with the other girls.

Myself and the girls watched the open mic, I felt that I could have been a stronger host, I didn't want to put the host I was watching down, I wanted to share my talents and shine. I mentioned to Danni over breakfast that I would love to host and before I knew what had happened, beautiful Natasha, the manager, floated over and offered me the opportunity to host on 2nd January 2014: well that was a fast manifestation. Super fast materialisation of my dream, that Island was a place where dreams seemed to show in reality very quickly.

The sun sparkled on the sea, creating crystals of light and I knew that miracles existed. New Year's was approaching. I joined Francesca, Jenni the scottish girl I had just connected with, Lena and Pixie to have an adventure. We decided to have some mushroom shakes to see in the New Year. We meditated and chanted on the beach to clear our vibes, ready to delve into the psychedelic realm.

Myself and the crew of girls got the shakes at Stone bar, a small bar on the edge of a cliff made with wood; there was a DJ at the front with a woman named Cherry serving the potions. The plan was to have a whole shake each but the girls only wanted a half, and myself and Jenni followed suit because we wanted to be on the same wavelength. We shared intentions and blessed the trip, then headed to Mama rock, a huge rose quartz on the edge of the jungle, by the sea, with a view of the mountains and the horizon.

After 30 minutes we started to experience physical and visual effects from the shakes: the mountain was breathing; I could see the aura of the trees; they glowed bright. Myself and Jenni lay close together. I saw colours flowing through our bodies, with euphoric tides of love. The essence of that island was made of ecstasy and we were flying on its tides.

We climbed over the bamboo bridge that was broken in parts, it led to the rocks up to Club Eden, a wooden dance floor with UV paintings hanging from the ceilings and the walls. The bar was on top of the rocks, with a view to look at the ocean while listening to uplifting house. That bar was so beautiful, I felt like I had reached another realm, a space of immense beauty, how did they create such a gorgeous bar? It was empty, we had the dance floor to ourselves. It was perfect: Eden was the best club I had been to in the world. People arrived and everyone was so beautiful; they danced like no-one was watching and as if everyone was watching. Freedom in their movements, the soul expressed through the body, cutting shapes, in love with the self. Dancing with acceptance, no one was wasted, everyone was kind, open and inviting, this was a welcomed energy especially while I was high.

We left to go up the cliff edge on small steps, heading to Guy's Bar. I had lost my shoes by this point: after a few days on the island I had become a bare-footed wanderer. I rapped to Jenni as we walked. Up at Guy's, we heard some bangs and saw some fireworks in the distance. Guys bar is set outside, a dance floor on the sand, with wooden seats to sit and chill. A view of the jungle, I held Jenni in my arms, even though she was so much taller. Time no longer counted; we were in the rhythm of the night; at the mercy of the jungle; nature was guiding us.

It was the best New Year's in such a long time. After giving up drinking and chemical highs I'd wondered if I would find the experience magical… and I did.

The night was over for us at 4.30am. Jenni and I stayed together. We went back to The Sanctuary nesteled under its roof. We made a nest of pillows, it was so cosy. We wrapped around each others' bodies, in a bubble, then fell asleep.
We woke early as the cafe needed to start business for the day. We ate energy balls and drank smoothies, on a health kick. We felt refreshed, the New Year was starting in beauty. It was a gorgeous day: Guy's bar played music that bounced the island all day. We visited Rhona, one of my buddhist leaders from Camden. Rhona supports a group of young women in faith in our area and I am one of the women she supports. Together we did New Year's Gongyo which is payers as part of Buddhist practise, where we recite two sections of the Lotus Sutra which is the teachings our practise is based on. We practised in Rhona's room, which happened to be just under ours. We

joined in unison, connecting our ceremony with the universe, setting intentions for world peace in the chant session. Afterwards, feeling at peace, myself and Jenni slept outside on a board of wood near one of the healing areas. We didn't have guests where we were staying and we were not yet ready to leave each other. We slept well outside that night, wrapped around each other. It was such a sweet moment.

*****

Rolling into the first show of 2015. It was the 2nd of Jan and now I actually had to run the open mic. I was nervous. Everyone I had met on this part of the Island would be there, all the teachers from all the classes I had been to, all the people I had met at the beach, at dinner, at the parties. My mind started to speak doubts to me: would people turn up? Did I just get ahead of myself, having so much bravado and balls that I put myself into a situation on a stage that I might not be ready for? This weren't like London promotion; there was no Facebook invite or flyers; no way of falling back on my regular routine to promote the show. What if the show was a total flop, what if none of the musicans made it to the open mic and it was dead and boring?

When the time came, I decided to open my heart to the flow of the event and step into it as a piece of the puzzle, letting go of control. The gig was instantly full. I gave each artist two songs and they strictly kept to the timing. The show was gorgeous. Hippies on a blanket on the floor hugged up together and the bar and tables fully booked. Each act was of a very high standard; there was so much talent in this community. The show was a success: my lesson here was to trust myself. I didn't need to push myself; I just needed to step into alignment with the intention, and all manifested perfectly.

The next morning we went on a jungle hike to the next beach, Haad Rin, for some dough. Lena and Pixie were wearing flip flops which weren't so helpful through the jungle. I was wearing shorts, which were equally unhelpful and I was bitten constantly by mosquitoes; reminders we were humans in Paradise. We hiked upwards for an hour, sweat dripping, finding the way by following markings on the trees: it was some adventure. The kind I'd always loved. At the top there was a look-out point. The world was so expansive from that height; Mother Nature so beautiful, so wise. The sea lay ahead, the horizon a blur, the water so clear against the sky. The jungle – green so richly green – went on as far as my eyes could see. The feeling of being so high up was inspiring. We continued the trek, the trees towering above. It was easier going down than up, though we had to take care not to slide.

We arrived at Haad Rin. It was so different to the community we had been a part of for the last couple of weeks. There were plenty of bars where the alcohol was poured into buckets for drinkers, and lots of cheap spirit. People not drinking alcohol, could maybe find a can of Coke or a fake Red Bull. We were judgmental and called the ravers bucket monsters.

The beach was rammed, full of sunburnt travellers. The roads were dirt tracks, the dust rose up as we walked. There were endless clothes shops, with each item between £3 - £10 for clothes of an OK quality, we bought some bits and pieces. I called my nieces in London as I'd missed their birthdays and Christmas Day. My older niece was surpried to hear from me, there was not a phone where I had been staying so I was a little late to call. It was so nice to hear her voice and to say 'Hi' to my sister, connect to my loved one's. We hung out for as long as we could bear it on the commercial side of the island before getting a taxi-boat back home. It was now dark and travelling on a small boat at night with quite a few people piled in, with just a small light ahead through the thick of the stormy night sea was more than a little scary. I couldn't see anything in front of the small patch of sea where the light shone, the boat constantly rocked with the waves crashing onto us. I planned in my head how to survive if the boat tipped up, and wondered what creatures lived in the sea there – God only knew. I might make a nice munch if sharks were about. Thankfully, we arrived home to our magic spot back at The Sanctuary safe and sound.

*****

The days there were mellow: we danced, wrote poetry, painted, read, meditated, swam and chilled; we were happy and the conversations were electric. I still wanted to get a tattoo. I made a pact with myself that if I had enough money in my account, I'd get it done. I checked with my bank, and my work had paid me £130 from leftover holiday pay, I had quit my bar job before making my way to the island.

Pixie styled the letters NMRK for the tattoo I'd decided to get on my fingers. NMRK stands for Nam Moyho Renge Kyo, it is the words we chant as part of our practise. They are the title of the final 28 chapters of the Lotus Sutra which we believe are the most powerful sutras as these are the sutras that state every being has buddhahood. It is a life condition you can reveal through chanting. Everyone has the power to become enlightened as much as anyone else, the Sutra teaches we are all equal. The end of each letter of my tattoo was to be curled, like the tips of musical notes. There was a tattoo artist who was part of the community so I booked in with him. It was the equivalent of £60 for the tattoo which weren't that cheap; in fact it was kinda similar to London prices.

Dean, the tattoo artist, must have been in his early to mid-40s, with a fashionable hair cut, all funky and different. His face was kind; he had smiles etched into his skin. He was from South Africa, but his accent was a soft mix of all the countries he had frequented: he was a man of the world and belonged to no one space. We marked out the letters on my skin, he took a crystal out of his pouch and blessed it, then tied a needle to the crystal. We were having deep conversations and he then started a ceremony before getting to work.

We sat facing each other cross-legged and held strong eye contact; we did some breathing techniques and chants led by him. His eyes seemed to float and I no longer saw his face. I felt his heartbeat in a rhythm: I don't fancy men much but in that moment I felt intense love and was kinda wishing he would lay me down and make love to me. Even though I don't feel this very often with men, I felt it strongly in that moment. He laid me down on a mat with a pillow, burned incense all around us, then rested my hand on a heart-shaped pillow.

The act of tattooing didn't hurt at all. It took two hours to ink my skin, but with the ceremony the whole process took four hours. As we said goodbye I said, 'I love you'. He said it back; we hugged and walked in opposite directions. I've not seen him since.

Jenny and I had our last night at Eden bar, dancing with our friends, feeling the love. My tattoo looked so feminine. I had always thought that finger tattoos would have a masculine feel to them but my body art is soft and fluid.

The next morning we linked up with the girls in the bar for breakfast. Pixie was crying, saying she didn't want to leave. She decided to change her ticket. Lena and I were ready to get back to our London lives, but first we had booked a night in Bangkok. Over breakfast Jenni was so sweet, we ate some delicious fruits, Francessa our other good friend was having smoothies as it was her day for just liquids. As we sat for the last time I was so ready to leave, I was dying to get to a faster paced environment. It was difficult to leave our friends who loved this spot so much. The taxi boat was waiting, if we didn't get on it we would be waiting until the night for the next one or paying a big heap of money. We jumped in the boat, myself and Lena as Pixie stayed behind, Jennie and Pixie ran into the sea waving us off as we prepared for the next leg of our adventure.

*****

Back on the long night bus. I weren't scared this time when we were dropped in the middle of nowhere. This was part of the adventure and I knew we would get to Bangkok so surrendered to the process of getting there. Three weeks in Paradise has an effect on you. When we arrived it was sickly hot in the city, the smell was strong, a mix of fish and noodles with meats I didn't recognise. We walked through Khao San Road, a busy market, looking for places to stay for the night and to drop off our bags, but most of the spots were full. After the fifth or sixth place, we managed to get a room for the night. The hotel weren't the best; we had a small room with a bed we shared. We grabbed some sleep, a cold shower and headed out.

Ladyboys stood in front of bars, the constant beeping of cars and bikes once again the soundtrack to the day. This was our shopping opportunity after being in a bubble in a secret spot on a paradise island for the past three weeks. We got gifts for friends and family back home, and we explored a little, but I was less than happy: I don't find shopping fun, plus it was hot and I weren't used to the smells, food I didn't recognise, fumes from the cars which now smelt different, mixed with the sent of the alochol from the bars that lined the street. Each spot was a bar, a restaurent, a clothes or ornaments shop for tourists and the roads had side roads where the hotels were.

We got back to our room for the night and settled in, but I felt scared: the noises were loud and threatening, we had been in such a quiet space in the jungle in Paradise but now it actually felt like we were in a foriegn place. Cars beeping, people shouting, movment in the corridors of where we were staying, then someone banged on our door hard in the night while running past. Eventually we got to sleep, but had to wake at 5.30am to catch the bus to the airport.

We stood on the now deserted road waiting for the bus to arrive, with no idea if we'd been ripped off for our tickets, but also not caring as long as we made our flight in time. All was blessed however, as just then the bus arrived and we made it to the airport and with time to spare.

Once again we had to change flights in Bahrain – a 21 hour stop-over this time. It was the most frustrating airport ever: no wifi, the internet didn't work on the old skool machines, and we kept getting kicked out of the gadget shops for using the tablets to try and check our mail. We went down to where the flight had come in to find out from the staff what we could do, but were dismissed. We did look scruffy; my trainers were musty and my tie-dye top weren't going down well.

We went to a customer information point to complain about how we'd been treated. We were told we were treated badly because of how we looked, and were offered a hotel room for £30 each to make up for the rude treatment. At first I was like, hell no: we were worth more than that and I weren't welcoming that sort of attitude into my life. But after an hour of trying to sleep in the airport with the bright lights and super uncomfortable chairs, we took it.

The hotel was worth every penny. We slept a few hours in a bed, had a shower and a breakfast and then were dropped back to the airport, only to find that our plane had been delayed. Lena was her usual joyful self. She maintained a typical lightness and good cheer even though she was tired. I wished I could find her positive attitude in myself, but at that moment I was straight-up miserable. Lena made it her mission to keep me occupied: we bought books and I decided to make the best out of the situation. Eventually it was time to board, and from then onwards it almost felt like we blinked and were in London.

Everything felt so different back home, back to the grey city, back to being on a fast tube. When I got to my stop, looking at the adverts all over the station was almost too much for me but I love London: it is my true home. My multi-coloured flat welcomed me, as did my cats. Oh it was so good to be back... But what a trip. I was determined to get my life on track. I started to apply for youth work jobs. Pixie stayed another two months on the Island doing a huge graffiti mural with Jenni. Jenni travelled to India then back to London to stay with me for 10 days before she went home to Scotland. Jenni was such an awesome guest, we had the most perfect time together. Jenni is more than a friend now she is a sister, she also remains in close contact with Danni, Francessca, Lena and

Pixie. The tribe keeps expanding, Jenni hoop danced for the LC Collective album launch and Pixie did the graffiti art back in May 2015. Lasting friendships and creative relationships.

Foster Care

I'd woken up late, heart beating out of my chest, knowing today was the day. Fuck, how could I be late? Off all the times to sleep more… What use was more sleep to my family's life there and then?

I had been having meetings with Social Services, putting myself forward to become the official carer of my younger brother, aged 14, and my sister, aged 13; I was 19. My other brother 17 was unwell at the time and he was to be sectioned. My siblings all lived at my mum's at this point while I had been living at my dad's druggy flat in Dalston. Social Services would rehome the other 2 with me. Mum had gone past being able to care for her children; the system was all that was left and I wanted to do anything I could in my power to keep my family together. Fuck them all going into care, that's too fucked, I truley believed I could take care of them.

Social Services thought that me standing in was a good idea without taking a look at the state of my mental health, or how we would work as a unit. I was good at talking and I guess the words I spoke were the solution they were looking for. I meant it with my heart but now see that I didn't really have the skills to care for two teenagers.

I made my way to my mum's in Camden; from my dad's place in Dalston, I had to bunk the train 'cause I didn't have any money. When I reached the flat she was drunk, as usual, the vibe in the house felt like walking across broken glass, each step a cut to the soul. I asked her where my siblings were. She said the Social Worker had taken them.

That moment, them words sliced like razor blades through my reality, shredding all I had ever known. I became hysterical:

HOW THE FUCK DID YOU LET HER TAKE THEM YOU FUCKING BITCH...

I had no kind words left.

FUCK YOU, FUCKING DRUNK SLAG...

How could you let them take your children? My little siblings taken by the Social Worker plus she was drinking. She'd been drunk for like ten years: fuck this woman.

I screamed and wanted to smash everything in sight but the house was so mashed it wouldn't make much difference. I looked out the window onto the estate, hoping to see them but nothing: just the same green, the same corner shop. How could I have been late and how could she have let this go down? Her kids were now victims to the system.

My mum's flat had become the local cotch: I would go there, all the boys would come up with drugs and we would pull the curtains, even on sunny days, and smoke. It werent ideal having all the boys in our flat but they always brought plenty of hash or skunk with them so we would let them in. We were smoking from 9am most days. Mum most times didn't come home so she didn't really know what was going on. The wallpaper in the living room had been pulled off on one side of the wall and all the boys had graffit'd the wall with proper shit tags and writing. Our house was a joke, with people marking territory that should have been our home. Now it was just a spot to get high. It still always felt more like home than my dad's though, even though it was at my dad's that I was sleeping at that time. It was at my mum's where I grew up. Now it was just some spot for everyone to plot and get mashed.

Social Services mainly got involved 'cause the younger ones never went school. I remembered Camden Girls' staff coming and knocking for my sister to get her to go to school. I think they alerted the Social Services. Mum had been to Social Services 'nuff times but no action was taken, they didn't pay attention to the woman begging for help when she needed it and asked for it. They gave us money for a day trip to Margate once: it was nice to see the sea but it weren't nice that our mum could no longer cope with being a mother.

We would run out of gas and electric for the flat and have no food. A couple of times I'd forge her signature to get her weekly dole money from the post office, take enough for the kids and give her the rest to spend, 'cause we needed the basics to get by. She weren't capable of the basics at this point in time, though. The drink had her, her demons now her best friends and meanwhile the Social Services had come to take my siblings from her hell straight into another one.

*****

I had never felt so much desperation and pain, knowing my siblings had been taken into care. The world was at its end. Then the doorbell rang. It was the Social Worker and my siblings: she had taken them for food, not to a placement, I was getting the opportunity to be there. We then packed my two youngest siblings' essentials and left my mum in the flat. We began our journey with me as their sole carer in a hotel near Holborn, a dingy place, dark and dirty, three of us in a small room with three single beds. It stank. We were all emotionally fucked. This was not like when we had been away together before: we had hardly any of our belongings, as they were still at Mum's place. We were told we were there for a night, not knowing our fate, with nowhere to cook and with nothing to do. No luxuries, barely even basics: just three teenagers in a room. I swear that boys weren't supposed to share with girls, even if they were siblings. What kinda madness was this?

After speaking to the guy at reception we were informed that the Social Worker had paid for a week's stay in advance. Why did she tell us it was just a day? We called the Social Worker from the phonebox, proper angry, just wanting to know what was going on. We felt so unsafe, so unhappy: like the blind leading the blind, we faced the darkness together. She assured us we would not be there for a week.

We got moved quicker cause we complained, we stayed there for like 4 days then we were moved to our new place, in Tottenham. We were given a house to stay in that gave us bread and cornflakes with milk, that's what a bed and breakfast is apparently. Social Services gave us keys and everything: imagine Social Services trusting three traumatised teenagers with a house. The place looked like it had been decorated by a granny like 50 years ago and she'd never changed a thing. But must have been a frosty granny, 'cause there was no feelings of love in those rooms.

We had a living room, a dining room, kitchen, small garden,

and upstairs there were three rooms. We had a small busted TV that only worked with a hanger out the back as an aerial. All our clothes and belongings were in black bags, and our lives felt like rubbish: it feels like a cruel joke when things so accurately symbolize your life. Nothing about this was funny: it was real and it weren't cool.

What were we to do? We had £100 a week to live on between us. My younger brother and sister got their bus passes paid for, but it took an hour to and from school every day. I had to manage my life with my part time job at Sainsburys in Dalston and looking after the kids. It was crazy; we were so far from any of our social and support networks; we were living in an area that we had never been to before. Back then even 30 minutes from home felt like another country: here we were, Camden kids in Tottenham. This was long.

We didn't know what to do with our time, so we would make up comedy shows, mimicking our parents. If you don't laugh, you cry, and this was our coping mechanism. A policewoman came over one time with our Social Worker, asking us to prosecute our mum. It was kinda crazy, 'cause we just loved her so much, no matter what she had done. I was imagining her in jail then coming out without a flat, living in hostels; it didn't seem right. We said no: we still defended her, even though we also felt so angry.

Working part-time at Sainsbury's in Dalston didn't last long 'cause my siblings would fight every time I left the house; serious fights. I would have to come home to sort them out. I cooked, did the cleaning, and washed the clothes... I wanted so much to make our family functional, yet my understanding of family was so distorted: creating a happy home was what you did on TV shows, and this was reality.

After a couple of months our other brother 17 got taken from Mum, too: just as well really as he was drinking and smoking every day. A couple of times he smoked crack with one of Mum's boyfriends. He was willing to do anything for a buzz and it was landing him in trouble with the police. Then he was sectioned 'cause the voices were taking over his daily life. I dont know if the drugs caused his mental health or if it was always there, I guess I will never know. That's what our family had become: me and my youngest siblings in Tottenham; my other brother in hospital; Mum drunk in Camden; Dad scagged out in Dalston. It was a challenge to keep our heads up, the pillars holding up any sense of reality were crumbling all around us.

During this time I was becoming super curious about my sexuality: boys weren't doing it for me, and I needed to know how I felt being with a girl. I was tryna be the carer to two of my siblings, visit my other bro in hospital, and at the same time explore who I was in my tainted world.

We lived in Tottenham for a while but I was struggling to cope as the carer, so Social Services called an an emergency family meeting in Ireland. Its purpose was to see who could become the carer for my younger brother and sister, 'cause I was losing my grip. I was trying to hold on with all the life I had but it was like trying to hold on to rubble at the top of a cliff; my fall was inevitable. We flew over, I flew with my younger brother, my sister flew over with my dad. The meeting had the majority of our family there, our dad as well as 7 Aunties and 2 Uncles all from Ireland, with a couple of the family who lived in England. Silla Carron from our local estate, a woman who lived downstairs and always looked out for my sister had made it over, even though she was disabled and travelling was an issue for her.

We were all gathered in a hotel conference room, the family and the extended family members. Most of it is a blur as it was such a strange experience. Our Social Worker led the meeting, we were sitting in a room full of strangers, all these family members who had been a huge part of our childhood were now strangers. Silla offered my sister a home, there was not any solution found for my younger brother, my other brother was still in hospital having been sectioned.

Silla wanted to take my sister in, as did one of our aunties. I had looked after my sister for six months. I wanted nothing more than to do a good job, but I had been trained by failures, so I walked the same path. Silla offered some stability for my sister: my sister moved back to Camden from our place in Tottenham, at least she was back in her local area, with her friends and familiarities. Silla's house was in the same block as our mum's. It must have been weird to live there; in the same place yet at the same time, a totally different space. Must have been really hard for my sister to live downstairs to our mum and still see her going past. There weren't many other options, I had gone as far as I could as a career.

On a very painful day a few months after the Ireland meeting I faced my younger brother with the news that we couldn't stay in the situation we were in any longer.. I wanted to keep things as they were, but I could feel my mental health deteriorating and I knew I had to focus on my growth so I could be an example, instead of us crumbling together. Our home became an emotional freezer, with him disappearing all weekend and hating me – as he was entitled to. It was easier to hate than love, when all around you had let you down. I had become another person that had let him down. A month later he was placed In his first foster home. I helped him to move to a strangers home in some far area from his school (again), and we went on our seperate journeys.

I moved to Cornwall for six weeks that summer. I packed my bags, bought a tent with a cheque that had no money to back it up, and lived in a field and worked in a pub. I loved my tent with just a shower block nearby to wash in. It was half an hour's walk to the sea.

I finally had time to try and discover myself, and work through my mental illness and pain. It broke my heart to leave my family, I was so lost I didn't know what else I could do. I decided to set out on a journey to try and find myself. Maybe, just maybe, if I found myself, I could lead the way for my sister and brothers, and really achieve it.

Fuck the Pain Away

I'd got so sick of wanting to fuck the pain away, a silly pattern of behaviour I accustomed myself to; passing my rejection onto another being, as if my fingertips on another pussy would be the superglue for my broken heart. My mother's promiscuous lifestyle emulated in mine: yes, so Freudian to blame the parents. Having decided with my latest great love that it was time for 'space', my brain wandered through the little black book in my head, thinking who to shag, or where to go out on the pull: same old routine.

The one I was having 'space' from texted, and straight after, my phone rang: a pole dancer I knew had got me a job as an extra in a Danny Dyer film as a girl kissing another girl. The universe works quickly. Maybe it was a test to see whether space really was what I wanted: a paid job being half naked in provocative clothes with strippers. I spent all night tossing and turning, angel and devil on either shoulder, chatting strong. A moral dilemma. I didn't get much sleep.

When I reached the shoot I realised I weren't going to be

kissing the girl I had picked out in my head, my friend's hot backing dancer, but some weird chick with a fucked wig – some wig that had been worn for way too long. You can't re-erect that shit; it ain't pizza from yesterday; the oven won't help it. Her girlfriend was at the shoot and they looked like twins, from the bad clothes to the mashed up wigs: two chicks, one tall with surgically enhanced breasts, the other covered in amazing tattoos. Usually I'd find that style of woman hot, or interesting at least, but not today, not these two women purring at each other every two seconds.

Luckily some real talent arrived on the set, Tamara, a long-term friend (mixed-race girl, small with an amazing body; a talented burlesque performer), her stripper friend Alana (blonde, slim, beautiful) and Christina (a buff lesbian). We got hair and make-up done, stripped and put on our stripper outfits, then we had to oil our skin for the cameras. It was overtly sexy: Tamara got me to oil her luscious body, my hands between her thighs, running over her breasts. So delicious I wanted to eat her right there. Then she rubbed me down. While she was doing that, Christina asked me to rub oil over her back and hips, so I oiled her while having oil rubbed all over my body. It was actually heaven. Half-naked with goddesses: life does give us gifts at times.

After lunch we got on set. Danny Dyer was playing a gangster, a real rough character. We were playing girls auditioning to dance in his club. We started by lining up the scene. One of the women in a bad wig was on stage with me. We were told that we didn't have to kiss, but simulate oral sex. I was down with it but the bad wig woman who was suppose to be doing it with me wouldn't show her breasts so she was cut from the scene. Bring on Alana.... Buff ting. Tits worth four-and-a-half grand. I got on my knees in front of a room of hot girls. Alana took down her top, her succulent nipples right in my face, then grabbed my head and put it between her thighs, my face in her lacy knickers. An entrance into a sacred land, feeling lucky to be welcomed to such a paradise, even if it was only acting. We ran the scene like 15 times, breasts out, head in pussy. I did start to get really turned on.

Upstairs during a break, I was sitting next to Christina, still half-naked, in a sexually charged atmosphere. Tamara came over and gave us a lap dance. Was this even real? One of the butters girls on set called Karen had to take off her skirt; her baggy knickers were hanging, with an unkempt pussy on display. The whole place was cracking up. Bitchy strippers.

When I got home I let the whole day unfold in my mind. Looking back on it, I felt quite uncomfortable about the role I had to play. I don't enjoy being part of an exhibition or turning on men. Tamara was an artist, a professional in her game; flirty, chatty, stunning and took off the least amount of clothes (yet ironically still hypnotised the men); I admired her skill but most of all I admired her class. That day taught me plenty: fucking the pain away was not going to help ease my mind.

Uncle X

I'd always hated him, but I never really knew why; my childhood instinct was strong. He never liked me either: I had a loud-mouthed London accent and wouldn't give him my time; blonde, skinny, small, pretty and gobby. He didn't have a hold on me, a hold he was used to getting with girls. He was short, but from the height of a child looked tall; he had brown hair, cut in the style of a weirdo; wore those nerd glasses that everyone likes to rock right now, hillbilly glasses.

I think I was ten when I noticed that I really didn't like him – hated him, more like.

To look at his family anyone would have thought they were a normal family: house in the suburbs, two kids, a pretty wife... They had a detached place just outside of Dublin, located in a semicircle of houses, with lots of nice families that liked to play out and hang out in each other's homes. He was into Go-karting with his wife. I never got to see a Go-kart, but saw the pictures hanging up as proud moments in the hallway.

It all seemed normal, but felt fucked up, somehow. I was too young to understand why at that time, being 10 years old. I was 13 when I found out that he was a paedophile. Mum called me into the living room. She was sitting in front of one of the old gas fires. I remember, she sat me down, saying, 'Shauna, I have something to tell you.' She asked if I had been touched by him, but he never got close enough – I didn't like him.

My cousin, little cousin in Ireland had been subjected to years of sexual abuse by her father – my uncle. I didn't know how to process this information, barely a teenager myself at that point. Movies flashed in my mind, moments of when I could have realised what was going on, but I was a child and didn't know how to put that information together.

Suddenly, in front of the fireplace with Mum, memories made sense; memories that were once shiny happy ones were now tainted.

*****

We went to Ireland one summer, that summer was a strange one: I had a big fight with my Uncle X cause I accidently broke his soda-stream maker. I was outside the house on the porch and he gave me a stern speaking to. From that moment on I hated him. I told Mum I hated him; what a fuck-head I thought.

He took us up a mountain. Mum loved the heather and the lavender, and kept stopping to tell us about the flowers. I was game for the challenge of the climb, but my youngest sister cried every step of the way. She was only a very little kid, so I couldn't really fault her. I loved climbing to the top, escaping the pathway that went round the mountain to go through the bushes straight up instead. The view from the top was incredible: we could see the sea, and the world looked like it was made out of plastic cause everything was so small, It all looked fake from that high up. The perspective shifted reality, I had never seen the world in that way. It was like a paradise. That was one of the last happy times we had in Ireland.

On the way home, my sister, my cousin and I were in the boot of the car – it was a Volvo and the boot could fit kids in. The seats from the back of the car folded back and it had pleantly of room for us to sit comfotably. Back in them days, there weren't so many seat belt rules. We fell asleep on the way back and when we woke up we were at the shopping mall, in a big car park. It was hot, so we opened the boot of the car and hung our feet out the door. My brother and boy cousin were standing at the back of the car. My cousin shut the car boot, without knowing that my foot was still hanging out of the door, trapping my toe in the catch, the lock of the boot. I was screaming but no one paid attention, everyone got into the car and my Uncle X started to drive. I was screaming for him to stop. He finally stopped and opened the boot of the car. Blood was pouring out of my toe. I couldn't believe what had happened. My head spun; screaming seemed to be the only way to stop the pain.

That night at the hospital, Mum joked with the nurses, saying she hoped she never saw them again: that was her little joke. The next day, I sat at home with my foot up, reading *The Twits* by Roald Dahl. I was bored sitting alone while the other kids played outside. I just wanted to go out and join in the fun. I convinced Mum to let me out. I got on the bike with my cousin on the back; we raced my brother; the bike fell and my cousin and I started crying.

I ended up back in the hospital. I had dislocated my right thumb and fractured it in two places. I stayed overnight so I would be ready for an operation the next day. One of my other aunties worked at the hospital. It was nice to see her smiling face as I was put to sleep. I woke with a strong cast on my arm, and couldn't stop throwing up after the anaesthetic.

When I look back now, I think it was no coincidence that I had two serious accidents in 24 hours while being in that house and energy. It is as if I was trying to let the adults know what I was feeling: I could tell things weren't right, but didn't understand what was wrong. I didn't know how to express a feeling I couldn't describe.

The truth about Uncle X tore my mum's family apart when it came out. He had been caught. It went to court, and he was sentenced to ten years. He was locked up.

Mum hit the drink bad after all this came out. There were no more holidays to Ireland. A once massive but close family was left in tatters: the curse of sexual abuse. My mum's family is still recovering, twenty years on. Abuse is a life destroyer.

Dippy the Dog

Dippy was my childhood dog and became the best beggar in Camden, a scruffy mongrel from a family of mongrels belonging to some New Age travellers. You can recognise the hippy's breed of dog; they usually belong to a Crusty – you know, them scruffy people, usually white, with matted dreadlocks and baggy army pants, often some big silver piercings. Their dogs are usually on a rope looped around the neck or running free. Dippy ran free through the drunks and trash-cans; she knew the streets of Camden better than any human.

This dog had lived a rough life and it showed: she could have got a job modelling for the RSPCA adverts. Just £2 a month can make such a change. Dippy had one good eye, the other was blind; her fur, once so shiny, had turned matted with grey streaks running all over her tiny frame. Such a character was this little dog, with a loud bark and a sharp bite. Not one to be messed with.

I would walk with her in Camden. All the punks knew her, calling to her as she would run, tail wagging, distributing flying licks. She was more popular than me! Lucky I wasn't insecure or I might have got jealous. Because my mum was drunk so often the dog's dinner would also get forgotten. So Dippy learned to survive on the fast-food-paved streets of Camden. She would sit next to her chosen target, look up with the one eye that worked and the other eye shining hollow; waiting silently, looking so wounded, following every bite sorrowfully, without breaking concentration.

She could spark a flame in the iciest of hearts, or maybe the guilt of leaving a mutt starving is too much for people. Either way, the dog was a champion. An avid Stella drinker, she knew the can: anyone drinking Stella would be watched like a hawk. The minute the can got put down she would knock it over with her paw then drink her rewards. So much skill.

She was lost by random drunks, went missing for days, but always found her way back to Castle Road, our old family home. Her body after 15 years of life, fighting and surviving a storm of events that would kill most humans was starting to give way; but her vicious streak was stronger than ever. I suppose after a while you bite back.

She was loved so much as a family dog, best friends with all four of us children. I bet she missed the family when we had left and she became a street dog. I missed her.

I heard she had to be put down; it was time for her soul to leave her hairy frame. Bye, Dippy you legend. You were the best dog, and Camden will never forget you.

Two Worlds in a Day

I work in two youth clubs, both in East London; both the areas surrounding the clubs are notorious for gang violence. One of them I work in on a Wednesday, which can be challenging as once a month I also have Morning Gloryville, a sobriety movement where people get together for a massive sober rave in the early hours. I'm the resident emcee at Morning Gloryville which means once a month, I go to Morning Gloryville, have a few hours off, then do a youth workshop in East London in the evening.

One particular Wednesday like this, a boy brought in a machete to the youth club I was working at in the evening: man that experience messed me up. I was traumatised to my core. My physical being reacted with shock. All I kept thinking after was imagine how the kids feel, being subjected to violence as a normality?

The morning had started with my heart being blown up amongst 800 sober ravers, jamming with one of my best friends I hardly ever see, a couple of cups of cacao and a long shift on the mic. The experience was out of this world, so euphoric. The crowd was more up for it than any other crowd I have rocked the mic for: the lack of alcohol at Morning Gloryville seems to create a more open atmosphere; more love and more fun. I'm always super tired and tripped out after the event – it takes some next level energy rocking the mic at the rave; I have to travel out of my head and into my heart to connect with the crowd.

I had a nap, a chant and went to work at the youth club in East London. When I got there, there was sadness in the air: something had gone down in the play session; it was kept confidential and even I weren't allowed to know but I sensed that was for the best. The club started to fill up quickly, and the Gangs Unit were there to run a workshop. The club is located in the thick of the estate. When I came for my interview I couldn't find the place as it's behind the flats with a green at the back. Most the boys who go to the club can't go past the green as they have beef with the boys from the estate just past it.

A couple of the boys went into the ICT room and started to play rap videos. As a rapper, I don't rate the style of calling out beef with another area like in the videos they were watching: all that boasting about how much they have, compared to the others. I suppose that is just a symptom of poverty. When you have nothing, there's more of a need to tell everyone what you have.

I was helping the Gangs Unit guy set up the projector and letting all the young people in the centre know that the activities would be stopped while the workshop took place. A couple of the boys were starting to have an argument, one saying 'You don't back beef.' the next one replied, 'Nah, you don't do nothing: bring your boys.' The first one said, 'Make the call: do it' then the other left the club.

I had a feeling something big was going to go down but at that point it was no more than a typical argument often heard in the centre between two young men. One of the boys left then a little while later he walked in and opened his jacket to reveal a huge knife – a machete – in a sheath, stuffed in his clothes.

Fuck! I felt so scared in that moment. He was shouting and making for the boy he had been arguing with. The staff jumped up and got between the boys. I rate my manager; a strong female who stood up with the Gang Unit man and other staff who happened to be in the centre that day. It all went so fast it was a blur; I know they got both the boys outside the front door and all the men in the building helped break it up.

I got myself into the ICT room with the other young people – kids ranging from 13 to 17 years of age. The ICT room was safe as it can only be opened from the inside. The young people there were unphased. This sort of thing was just normal to them; beef kicking off like this.

The Gang Unit guy was still determined to run his workshop. Meanwhile outside the youth club the tension from the incident before was thick in the air and the boy with the machete was still hanging around. I reminded myself that we were safe inside, the man from the Gang Unit was now doing a presentation about youth who go to prison and end up joining Islamist extremist, getting their hands on more effective weapons than they previously owned, then going to other countries and blowing themselves up. The Gang Unit man's presentation also included a section on young women being groomed and the effect it was having on society. He showed disturbing images throughout the workshop to accompany his words. I was in a lulle already, tripped out after the incident with the young man and machete while the Gang Unit officer was insisting on showing us the worst case scenario for the kids that ended up in jail and became Islamist extremists. It all seemed a little strange but at this point I felt like I was in fight or flight mode and too busy trying to process what had just happened to give the Gang Unit presentation too much thought.

The youth club stayed open the rest of the day. The Gang Unit officer had left and taken the machete. But the boy who the knife belonged to kept walking into the club, acting like everything that had happened was normal. He asked for his knife back and was told, gently, that the Gang Unit officer had taken it.

To try to end the session on a positive note, we started kicking some freestyles in the office, which looked on to the reception area. A couple of the boys were dropping bars to a Drake beat, I dropped a verse about knife crime, they dropped a couple more verses, then I kicked an off-the-top-of-the-dome freestyle, with lyrics connected to their names, the club and life, with a dope flow; it impressed the boys. One of the boys was like, 'Rah, you're so good, how come you're not famous?' I said that it took more than just talent to be famous, and thanked him for the compliment.

The vibe wrapped up and our lead worker suggested shutting up early, though only by 20 minutes. I was happy at the request. We tidied up the building, the young people left and we started to write up the debrief for the evening.

Just as I started writing, the boy who had brought the machete came through the front door – it was broken so he was free to enter. He asked for his knife back again. We explained again that the Gang Unit officer had taken it and he threatened to smash the glass barrier which was separating us and to 'Smash us all up'. He said people wanted to kill him and he needs this knife for protection. I looked at this young black man, 17 years old, and I knew he was telling the truth: a few months back there had been a dangerous fight in the club 'cause some of the boys who were part of one gang went near some neighbouring gang's territory. The youth workers and youth clubs work tirelessly to provide a positive environment for the young people. The war on the streets is very real, the workers go above and beyond but sometimes the streets still flow into the club.

I didn't know what the fuck to do in this moment. Time seemed to freeze then suddenly a chair came crashing through the reception glass, landing a few inches away from me. I leapt up and ran to a space I thought might be safer. I thought he would jump over the counter and really go into fight mode. I was looking for a way out of the building, desperately searching for safety, in a terrifying situation. He ran out and left, the glass didn't fully break which was a miracle. Everyone was in shock, we closed down. I hoped and prayed that the young man was safe. I felt like his rage came from feeling at risk and that carrying that rage would only further put him at risk.

A member of the team dropped me to the station in his car, which was majorly appreciated. On the train my world spun in all directions I reached out to a Buddhist friend 'cause I needed some grounding after all that had happened. I didn't even reach my stop before the tears started – not just a couple of drops either, it was floods of emotions flowing out of my eyes. I reached home and let out a loud sob. It felt like a piping hot steel spike was piercing through my heart. I hadn't felt that kind of pain since my mum passed away.

I walked around my room and my flat, unsure of what was real, feeling like I was going to vomit. All I could think was that I had to encourage two young women in my Buddhist practise in the morning and how could I do that when I didn't believe that there was any hope for the planet in that moment.

Lucie, my co-leader from the SGI, called and we spoke for an hour: my sister-in-faith was always there for me. My sobbing continued. I don't understand this planet: why are we like this? Why are young men killing each other on the streets? The police were called by four different people to come and help when the incident kicked off but they never reached the 'hood'. All we had was one Gang Unit officer who happened to be there to do a presentation and who delivered the presentation, took the knife and then left. How could human life mean so little? I believe in world peace and understand my mission, but when faced with war, how realistic is that? Eventually I managed to calm down and fitted in a 20-minute chant before bed. I chanted for the boys' lives, chanted for their safety.

I woke early to chant again, my eyes were so swollen I looked like I had been punched. I ended up chanting with cucumbers on my eyes trying to fix up 'cause I had to go and encourage two young women. I kept digging to feel strength, digging deep 'cause I knew I couldn't give up just 'cause I had seen how real it is for these young people. That was just even more reason to continue.

The day before, Morning Gloryville had started the day with hope and helped me restore myself; seeing such beauty and magic and a way of raising the consciousness of the planet through dance. There were so many yoga teachers, healers and therapists in the room, dancing in social change through sober raving. That experience was such a sharp contrast to later that day where I was in the youth club surrounded by such aggression, violence and desperation, so much dispair.

Trying not to let the events of the day before defeat me, I went and did my home visits to the two young women I support in faith in the SGI. I went through the day fighting back tears in between the home visits, digging deep to a stronger part of myself that really does believe that winter can turn to spring for humanity. Every part of me wanted to shut down and run – maybe run off the face of the planet.

I had a spoken word workshop with a disengaged girls' group that evening for the Roundhouse at a local youth club as part of their outreach program. Roundhouse staff were visiting to see how it was going as the workshop had been hit and miss in terms of how many people showed up. I chanted before I left to go to it: we had a full house and got to do more of the project, which was great as I loved the girls I was working with.

After the workshop the next few days I had two back-to-back late night gigs. When they were over, I lay in darkness watching junk on my laptop, totally numb; the will to chant had left; I didn't feel able to summon any more strength in my life; I just wanted to numb the pain and exist in the empty space. The following morning it was the Morning Gloryville Christmas staff get together but I couldn't leave my place. I wanted so much to open my heart and join the celebration but I was paralysed and couldn't face human connection or to share any part of me after I had experienced such a traumatic event that week.

*****

I woke the next morning with the inspiration to chant, I had seen heaven and hell in the course of one day, and there must be reasons for this: the Buddhism I practise says there is meaning in everything. I fought my very low mood through my practice and started to regain the strength to go back to work. To say to the young people at the youth club that there is a life outside of the estate, and that they could create so much more for themselves. Re-inspiring myself is a constant journey, a journey in search of consistency, where I can create and share the light and hope with others. I fight on with my mentor Diasaku Ikeda, believing that we will enter a peaceful age on this planet; just knowing we probably won't see it in this lifetime.

Falling Out of Love the Right Way

She still beats in my heart; my mind carries our experiences through my life stream. Escaping the moment in a memory wave of love or hate, choosing how I want to view our experience. At times I revel in the beauty and my heart smiles as I relive lust-filled passion, but the next moment I remember all the reasons it didn't work out, the pain replacing the smile. I'm living a contradiction.

Love and hate are two sides of the same coin: but is it ever really love if it can be replaced by hate so quickly? Love turning into hate is the mind playing tricks on us, to hide the real meaning of what love is. Love is limitless, it knows no boundaries. Love has no conditions. When I think of the conditions of love that I place on how I want my partner to be, I know that isn't love. That's just a shopping list of how another can fit into my life.

Love is loving imperfections perfectly, seeing beyond behaviour patterns straight to the soul. Now we're not together, but I still really love her; I'm tryna hold onto the right frequency, not to let the negative thoughts occupy my mind space; to know love never dies, it's only the label of the relationship that changes.

I want to be so strong within myself, for my love for me to be so pure that I'm able to share my love with her no matter our situation. She's a goddess, a dazzling beauty: does she have to be in my arms for me to acknowledge her in this way? I want my love to be limitless, letting go of an egoist reality, recognising the full picture.

Each experience is a blessing. I bless each of her movements as a conscious being does, giving thanks for all that we have shared with a true intention. Though we parted with one part of our journey, we're ready to mature to the next. Accepting life's challenges with open arms, the only way is forward, embracing the change.

Getting Banged Up

Days were fading into darkness: I existed inside of bottles of drink and spliff ends. I would promise myself every night before going to sleep that this was the last time, but when the morning came I still didn't give a fuck about anything, so once again would bun a zoot and drink. I was best friends with Hayley – she was as lost as me: we were sailing together on a rough sea in a captain-less ship. Misery loves company and our misery called to each other, and created more misery. We fuelled each other's madness; best friends who could egg each other on to do anything. I was 17 with no real care for anything; a life with no love for self.

Hayley was small like me, mixed race and beautiful. She would scrape back her hair into a ponytail, rock tracksuits with those big gold earrings that rip your earholes downwards. She spoke fast and always said 'Definitely? You will be there, definitely, won't you?'

One day she came and linked up with me in Dalston; we bopped to Kingsland shopping centre, walked into Iceland supermarket. Hayley calmly picked up a bottle of champagne and walked out. I followed her, as I always did, also picked up a bottle and walked out behind her. We got back to my Dad's flat and popped open a bottle, celebrating what? I don't know. I pulled out a joint, one I had been saving to bun alone like a proper cat. I called in sick to work and we got the party going. My Dad's block is a block for junkies. We blazed out garage tunes, Hayley liked to MC along and always put me down anytime I would give it a go.

The bubbles fizzing through our minds, we bunked the train to Edgware where Hayley lived. We were gassed cause she had her own flat which to us meant let's have it up. It didn't matter that it was Wednesday: we were always up for getting mashed. On the way to hers we dropped into Marks and Spencer to nick another couple of bottles – we just picked them up and lifted them. My heart was pounding but I didn't really care about the consequences. We had both nicked a £40 big bottle each; we felt live when we had left the shop.

Hayley's house was a shrine to alcohol, lined with empty champagne bottles. She had been in the care system most of her life, but now she was in Semi-Independent accommodation, and a Social Worker would stay a couple of nights a week to make sure she was OK. Semi-Independent flats never felt quite like a home. I suppose 'cause a home needs love in it to make it a home. When you're broken, how can being out of your ends, far from all your family and friends give you the headspace to create love for a temporary home?

The phrase care system always struck me as kind of ironic as care is the missing ingredient. We drank and blazed most days 'cause we could do what we wanted at 17 years old. We thought we were living the dream, get fucked up as much as we could 'cause it was blessed.

Hayley's mate came round, another girl who was in the system, they met at a children's home some time back I think. We pumped out old skool garage though back then it weren't old skool – garage music had just started to break in the UK and we loved it. We danced and buss joke until all the magnums of champagne where gone. By the time we'd drunk them all, we were starving and I only had a quid for dinner.

We went on a rampage through the streets of Edgware. We ran into a kebab shop: they took so long to cook our chips that we knocked all the salad on the counter to the floor, cracking up, then running from the shop in case anyone caught up with us. Like Tasmanian devils we spun into storm clouds of drunken rage, knocking stuff over in shops, wreaking havoc everywhere we went.

Eventually we ended up in McDonald's. I ordered a burger and some chips after Hayley said she would lend me some money, and just as I paid, Hayley jumped over the counter to nick money from the till and then ran out of the place. The guy serving us ran after her and got the money back. I was frozen to the spot. Apart from the shock of what Hayley had done, I was really hungry and just wanted my food. I waited, my directionless life ground to a halt as I stood, static. When the police arrived I explained that I weren't a part of the drama and that I was just waiting for my food.

Two male offices dragged me onto the street; no talking, no reasoning, no listening. I dropped my phone, which was a contract phone, and I asked to pick it up, but was ignored. Hands behind my back in cuffs, I was bundled into the car. The summer night's fun was now a nightmare. I was screaming and crying, rage – scared at entering the unknown. We reached the station. Hayley's mate had been nicked, but Hayley herself weren't anywhere to be seen.

They took my shoe laces and anything else I had on me so I couldn't self-harm when in the cell. I got booked in for drunk and disorderly behaviour, and then thrown in a cell. I went nuts; I was kicking and screaming, punching the walls, throwing the mattress around the place; tryna beat the pain and rage out of my soul.

I was brought to see the psych doctor – I told him that I was going to kill myself, that I had aborted a baby just two months before and I hadn't told anyone. It might sound like a story I was spinning for the police but actually it was the truth. I told the doctor that if I could kill my baby I could kill myself and who cared? What did life matter? Just get the fuck away from me.

They made the decision to section me and called my Dad at the same time. He was living at Mum's at the time with my bothers and sisters 'cause Mum had run away to live with one of her mates.

Dad arrived in a cab from Camden with my sister before the psych team arrived. I confessed to my dad about the abortion, which had been this mad little secret. The secret had eaten at my soul until it manifested into this mad situation. The rage and hurt within me was still raw from having gone through doing the abortion and being alone. It was too much for my soul to bear. This time my dad saved me; he sorted me out 'cause I was a few hours away from being sectioned. And who knows how different my story would be if that had happened.

Not that life changed much, I was still living at my dad's mashed down flat alone, our mum weren't about, there was no ground to stand on, no way to climb up and out of where I was, everyday it felt like I was sinking. I was thankful I weren't in hospital though 'cause that would have been a whole other set of problems to deal with. Fuck it life was dark enough, the few stars that beamed light here and there had a thread of hope, being sectioned at that time would have been lights out, a starless sky, blanketed in darkness.

My Brother

He screamed in the night, telling me with absolute conviction that the crackheads upstairs were doing voodoo on him. He was only 17 years old. There was a crack house above my dad's flat, which would get regularly raided and have junkies jumping into the garden out the window. Those people couldn't give a shit – they were too busy selling the pussy of some young addict for their next hit and chasing their tails to be putting voodoo on anyone. Yet he wouldn't believe me when I tried to explain this to him. His big blue eyes looked into mine, he was so lost. I try to shut off the love in my heart that I've had for him since I felt him grow inside our mother's tummy, to stop the pain of losing him as he loses touch with reality a little more every day.

Such a beautiful, sensitive soul, he feels the world more than most. A council estate upbringing weren't the best environment for nourishing him: him, a wild daisy living in a bed of nettles, daily getting stung by all around him. Bullied in primary school, tortured in secondary school and a target in the ends. Living on the estate was like a constant cage fight, with most these young men growing up without fathers in overcrowded areas. They had to punch their way to getting respect. My brother would be the punch bag that took the blow when a boy had to prove he could fight. My brother would stand there, get punched in the face then run home to his Playstation, escape into a world where he held the controls.

A lab rat, fed ecstasy aged 12 years old at a squat party by one of our mum's so-called friends, he smoked cannabis every day and was given all kinds of weird drugs by the boys on the estate. One time, the boys took him to woods outside London; they left him at some boy's house and fed him magic mushrooms for days. We would shout out the balcony to the boys, asking when he was coming home. Our mum, the estate drunk, never got an answer; our family was a joke to them. My brother was an outcast tryna fit in, thinking he was part of the gang, and not really clocking onto the fact they were just taking the piss out of him. He was getting caught for all kinds of stupid crimes with the boys from Castle Haven the estate where we grew up. He was on last chance probation, which scared me: prison would kill him.

Voices crept into the fragments of his mind, with no parents to hold him in our reality, the drugs emphasised all of his illusions. He was diagnosed as schizophrenic aged 17. Was it conditioning? Drug induced? Or would he always have had this illness? I battle with this daily. I just want to remember him when he was well and didn't function on government pills.

He was sectioned and institutionalised at the Florence Nightingale Adolescent Unit, which was mainly a place for rich teenagers who tried to kill themselves. A year of him living there, he was still emotionally scarred to the core. When he was realeased he was released into the lion's den, a hostel in Kentish Town, living with boys from the Estate who had bullied him. Boys whose lives had also led them to living in that hostel for one reason or another. Straight from a year in hospital to a hostel with the boys who had tormented him everyday for his whole life. It was like the unexpected twist in a Steven King novel; a never-ending nightmare. He weren't given any skills or any support but he was given a bag of perscription pills and doctor's appointments.

So angry with the system, he left the hostel with red hot rage burning through his chest. He moved in with our dad in his one-bedroom place, sleeping on a mattress on the floor in the living room, no room for himself.

The drugs changed his body shape beyond all recognition; he was the skinny boy who could eat what he wanted before but now his belly ballooned and his eyes became distant, an outward sign of his troubles. What was supposed to be few months living with our dad to get his feet on the ground turned into eight years.

My brother and my dad finally got a bigger place to live and he got a place at college studying as a chef; he was doing really well. Thinking the pills were no longer necessary, he stopped taking them. College finished and he had nothing to do with his time. This coupled with the fact that he had stopped taking his pills meant the demon voices occupied his mind once again. As the leaves began to fall from the trees, his sanity fell away from his mind. He became overly aggressive, wide-eyed – he almost seemed possessed. He kept starting on everyone as if getting revenge for the days on the estate when he couldn't stick up for himself and not understanding that now we were in our mid-twenties, we earned respect in different ways. It was as though he had just woken up from being a teenager and his mind hadn't moved forward, stuck in a mental time warp. He came to stay with me; he would pace the house at night, muttering to himself. I would hear him at the knife drawer. It was so scary: he weren't himself. One time I asked him a simple question he shouted at me in a demonic voice that I didn't recognise, saying that he was going to throw me through the ceiling. I was so terrified I ran from the house, a constant stream of tears burning my cheeks, a pain in my heart knowing he would be back in hospital in the next few hours. He went back to my dad's.

The next day, eight riot police stormed into my dad's place with shields, headgear; the lot. My brother left the house, his head hung down – all the neighbours watching – into the back of the meat wagon. Locked up in a psychiatric unit once again, a danger to himself and others. The last time he got banged up was six years before.

He spent his Christmas at the Joshua Ward in King's Cross. It was horrific seeing him in there: my heart shattered as I witnessed him pacing around the big white room with other disturbed men. We played a game of pool but he struggled with his concentration. I had to turn my face to hide my tears and force myself to keep them inside so I could present myself as the strong sister he needed to see on that day.

He's still ill today. I can only hope and believe that he can pull himself through this. He's such a precious soul; I love him and can feel his pain. I want a magic wand to heal his mind; I wish that he could find happiness. I have to stay strong and enjoy life as I have learnt to, but for the moment I mourn for my brother, praying that he will find his way back to peace of mind.

Twisted in an Illusion

the mind's a smokescreen: what's real amongst the confusion?
delusion of our own making;
days and years we be creating,
yet to ourselves lying and faking,
seeing what we want to see;
living the life we believe.
losing hours, slipping through days
in a daydream haze.
not present in the present, losing life's gifts in presents:
hell is the sentence,
to our souls we repent,
want to be saved, pray to the god we don't believe in most days.
working 9-5 ,commercial slaves,
smile on the outside while the heart breaks.
roads, paved thick, concreted, suffocate the green with grey
just so we can fasten our pace.
chat on msn, never see a face –
screen to screen communicate –
wires, numbers half-cyborg,
machines to do chores.
we separate with gates and locks,
fear controls our outlook

while love hides in the shadows.
happiness in designer clothes
or sew it seams
dmt nightly releases dreams
yet the readings from this mystic land we don't receive:
we're taught to remember what the teachers teach,
not so much to reach
to our youth,
who see through
a system, yet are not given
tools to escape, so they kill each other in the ghetto. a pain expression
yet cut back cut back
a career beyond crack
shotter so we gotta fight back,
new ways to find money for the streets
get the rich to sponsor creativity;
real freedom of speech.
a land of equality
is yet to be reached,
yet revolution isn't beyond reach.
gotta keep remembering the matrix:
slow down, listen to breath,
skin to skin, eye to eye; time to connect,
inner self reflect
then to our world project.

Poetry Is More Than Life To Me

Poetry and expression saved my life and gave me perspective and love for myself. All those years of being a teenager, hating life, wanting to die and wondering how I was ever going to get out of the dark places: that seemed a lifetime ago.

It all changed when I reached my twenties, and started getting into performance art. Writing my experiences down, sharing them and receiving applause – just the clapping of hands switched my vibration, turned my frown upside down. I am passionate about sharing the beautiful wisdom I have been so blessed to find, to share it with other young people, sharing what was my fate, and the negative mind-set I was once in.

Expressing oneself is so important: to release, to feel, to be heard and to be valued. As humans we're all trying to find our place, to understand who we are. I grew up in public, on mics and with audiences, I aired my life and received love back.

Red Jen believing in me created a massive ripple effect 'cause I shared that love and belief with so many other young people as a result. I ran a poetry event called 'Lyrically Challenged' at Passing Clouds, a well known venue in Dalston which like so many other important London venues, was recently closed down (despite our protests). Each month, I challeneged two poets to write a new piece on a theme set by me. One month the challenge was to write a piece on human trafficking. It all took place in the upstairs of Passing Clouds, its wooden floors stripped bare, with fairy lights all over the place; a bar that looked like a ship; sofas everywhere and a homely atmosphere.

To run a poetry event is to give people a voice, to let them be heard in a safe environment; to let them grow with love and without judgement. Words are power and collectively, when we join our minds together, we create a revolution. Collective consciousness is strength: bringing poets and free thinkers together changes our world; we feel the force of life and the force of our oneness, which is shared with so many people.

Sometimes I see life as a crossroads: I can walk down the street and see a shadow of myself, a ghost of who I could have been, walking parallel to me on the streets of London. I see a homeless girl, lost out of her mind on the roads tryna find her soul through drugs. And I walk in real life next to her, an MC, a poetess, an actress living a life with beautiful people. I feel grateful every day that I found this place, this wonderful world filled with magic, I'm still living in the blocks but I'm out of the cage.

London and life: a heaven or hell, depending on the glasses we wear for the day. I choose to see the love and beauty. Poetry and self-expression are the tools for me to find those things, to find that heaven; so poetry is more than words: it is my healer, it is my mother and father; it is love in my veins. I give thanks.

Missing Morning Love

Next door, Chris Lena's dad who I was living with at the time sang about only needing your love in a plural sense: I now know he was singing it about his dead mother, his recent hurt of her leaving cracking his voice as the melody rose through the house.

It makes me feel kinda superficial that I related it to Patricia before I realised the true meaning of his song. When it was an ordinary love song, it made sense to relate it to her. Patricia is special; a woman that carries a force of positive vibrations . She has a gypsy energy – she is the free spirit that landed into my life, bringing an air of hope, she is my sunrise on a paradise island.

I prided myself on having a heart made of stone at that time, carrying luggage from the past, using the bags to create bars and chains around my heart. Memories of early childhood rejection swam around my being reminding me that I shouldn't feel love. Yet here I was one morning when she weren't there, missing her; a dull space in my heart in the opening that had been created.

She'd been staying with me most nights and the lack of sleep was starting to take its toll, the excitement of new love, the chemistry so spellbinding; it is the biggest amphetamine around. I should have slept in and caught up on all the hours I'd been missing, yet I woke early, searching for her warm body, wanting to find the cuddles and kisses only we shared. The empty space and the emotions I put into it showed me that I had become a melted marshmallow: soft, mushy and sickly to some.

She saw her future as marriage, a life built with the love she chooses to share it with. I was just in Primary or Nursery school when it came to love: all I saw was a black space in my life when it came to long-term plans. I accepted her openness as inspiration, because I was becoming bored of running away from a true connection. A part of my subconscious called for a woman I could really love; someone I could learn about love with.

So many achievements in my 28 years of life, yet still I lacked sustainable love. But here I was. Usually my clothes would all have to match, from the colour of my shoes to the jewellery I wore, to my hats; kinda borderline OCD. Now I was leaving the house uncoordinated, hair like shit so I had time for that one more kiss.

Floating in a haze, not wanting to leave our private cloud, the bubble we created together. It was like the cars outside no longer existed; earth weren't there any more. We were just travelling through the realm of togetherness, souls feeling through the physical flesh… Explosive, delicious. Even writing this I lose my pace.

WHAT HAD HAPPENED TO ME?

I blush now when our love is mentioned by others, where once upon a time I would have brushed it off, disrespectful of the specialness shared. A disciplined mind now understands about creating realities from thought-patterns and I am the master of my ship; I will sail in the right direction.

No Inspiration Right Now

stormy clouds
wanna be over and out
all doubt
depression's back again.
i'm slackening into nothingness
mind's a blank mess
alive and dead,
motionless.
fuck I felt good this morning;
tonight I could jump off the building:
the void the void the void the void
to avoid, feelings so repetitive. I'm annoyed
ain't I learnt yet?
remember then forget
fuck it
done with this

I have to win. I'm beyond bored of losing the battle with myself; knowing what I am capable of then sitting in a void of depression that I created for myself. I started 2017 with a Buddhist activity 'cause I had finished 2016 on a high and then crashed, falling real bad in the first week of 2017. I fell ill and when I'm unwell it triggers my depression, so I didn't move for three days. I shut the curtains, gave up on being a vegan, watched a show and binge ate, all the while aware that this was making me feel worse. It becomes a void; a space where I feel nothingness. I blank out all the emotions that I should face and hate every part of myself in those moments.

I weren't aware of the depression before: it crept in, mainly starting to get really bad after my mum died. How could I think doing cocaine and drinking without sleeping or eating for three days was a good idea? The downs would last a week. I wouldn't move, and any plans I had made went out the window, all the life-force I had while high, a meaningless mirage when I had no strength to carry any of it through. Fuck. Being blind to my own setbacks has been so annoying but being aware of them and sitting inside of them is equally annoying.

Now I see my depression and know what it is, chanting has helped immensely; I'm starting to live a much healthier life. It's the ups and the downs that fuck with me. I was flying at the end of the year, then next I know I'm in bed, bingeing on a new substance of self-hate. It takes me days to get back on my feet and back in the strong rhythm. I feel embarrassed of myself even writing this. It seems so pathetic when I always love to show how strong I am and how much I can transform any situation: I feel like a fake.

Monday in bed, Tuesday in bed, Wednesday moving a little;

Thursday I manage to chant and clean my place, do some exercise, get some business sorted and go to a gig I'm performing at with a date. My date says she's more depressed than I am. We go to a yoga class together and have a sauna. I sink pretty low when I get home, but manage to cook, which is good. I sit to chant and feel this inner fight happen: I can hear myself wanting to win and then I shut down. I lie on my bed for the rest of the night not doing a thing and just want to sleep so that the day is over. I have had enough. I get to sleep at 9.30pm. On Saturday I manage to have a good morning: I look after my friend's children and force myself out for the night, 'cause I don't need any more rest and I'm feeling totally antisocial.

Living in a soundproof room that I created, I scream inside in silence 'cause I don't want the world to know my pain. I don't want people to know that I can feel the most immense amount of love and inspiration on stage and feel awkward at a party, or not want to connect with people at all. And at the same time I want to build connections. There are a thousand versions of me all wanting to be expressed. I want to be inspired, to write every day for hours, to lose the time in expression, but those days feel like they have disappeared when I'm just lying there and can't write and can't face who I am.

Fuck, I am determined to make 2017 a different year for myself, 'cause these highs and lows and self-hate-filled days are fucking with my flow. I just keep getting back up and using the ground I fall on to push me up. How can I start a day full of joy and lose my steam halfway through? It used to be a week or months that I would lose to depression but the gap is getting smaller. Am I my coach or my critic? I feel emo writing this: looking at this part of myself is so uncomfortable.

I have tears in my eyes right now, sitting in a trendy Dalston cafe. If I spoke to you, my soul would shine; I would present the me that I want to be seen and bury my darkness for when I shut my curtains. I know what I can do, my talents and my gifts, but I don't feed them, I starve them and get so cut up and caught up.

We humans are such creatures of habit and patterns – the spiral spins, up and down I slide, up and down my board game: messed up, a survivor of childhood abuse. It's about being able to function for the rest of a day after being hit with a memory; to know it's the past and to be able to get on with whatever I am doing in the present, without a sinking feeling of doom.

Tonight I'm gonna go to Primrose Hill to watch the moon and gather energy from Mother Earth. Before I thought I needed to be indoors but it is the opposite: I need to be outside; I need to connect with others, and not just at events that I perform at. I'm working on finding the joy in each moment, learning to return to the moment without being hit by the fall-back. I'm working on knowing how lucky I am that I have a roof, that I have come so far and not to compare myself to others; to be kind and compassionate to myself so I can see when my triggers hit and deal with them gracefully; to be able to get up, 'cause when I kick myself it is harder to recover; to learn and keep moving forward, even when I take six steps back; to be compassionate; not to shout and scream; to deal with my bad habits and to start with the good habits again. And again, 'cause it all takes time and I'm working it out bit by bit. I give myself this speech when I'm in the thick of it. Well, I do give myself the speech but at those times it's like I'm trapped in water under a thick piece of ice; it's cold and scary, but if I keep going the ice begins to break.

Fuck I'm scared of my light and I'm scared of my dark and I'm scared to see how beautiful I really am; how much of my heart I can really share, how far and wide my positive influence can reach. All this is from the head, not the heart, and it is the heart that is important, the heart owns my soul's wisdom. And I'm full of wisdom and I am also a complete fool, tapping into my strengths and bringing my weakness to the surface, loving them both because they are a part of me. Knowing I am worthy of love.

Don't give up, don't give up girl, Shauna: there is so much more! Keep fighting and the flow will find me again: I will step into it!

Simon

I was either 12 or 13 when my mum started to see Simon: he was 26, her first serious toy boy. Mum had met him at Uni, she was tryna gain back a youth she felt she had lost to childbirth and four children. She was very proud of him and almost immediately invited him to live in our home. Simon fancied himself, with his skintight black leather pants, Superman-tight t-shirt, shoulder length curly hair and a goatee beard. He really did consider himself a gift to women, with a camp attitude, he was also bisexual which made my mum feel even more alternative and special, super liberal house we had out here.

They thought they were so rock 'n' roll, him and my mum licking tongues at any given opportunity, the Bonnie and Clyde of Camden, except they weren't robbers, just associating themselves with great love stories of our time. He was just another case of the heavy breath pants and sexual cries that echoed through our small flat in the dead of the night.

Simon had a gothic edge: he introduced us to lots of cinema. His look was inspired by Brandon Lee in *The Crow*. We watched that film so many times, as well as *The Rocky Horror Picture Show*, which became a family favourite. He cross-dressed and blurred the gender norms: my mum was in heaven proper loving this guy.

At 13 I was fully developed, round breasts, long natural blonde hair, with a tiny waist. I didn't know I was beautiful because no-one had ever told me or helped me to understand how to deal with developing into a woman. My mum would call me a vain bitch when I looked in the mirror.

In the midst of this confusion, I could feel his eyes on me and I didn't like it at all. I didn't like to hug him or be affectionate; I was OK with that with a good few of my mum's friends, but not him.

Our mum was particulalrly losing her hold on reality at this time, the drink, the drugs, the bohemian life was her world, not the family home. If she was home she was drinking on a daily basis – mainly beers but at times I would check her bag and find little vodka bottles. I always thought it was the same bottle.

When Mum was in the pub, Simon would stay home with us. We would be naughty. Simon was getting into the flow with our family and following suit with the violence he witnessed with our mum. I clearly remember the first time he got violent in the home. It was with my brother. We were annoyed that our mum didn't come home but were too young to understand or verbally express this, so it would come out in bad behaviour. My bro got rude, Simon ran after him to his room and gave him a spanking on his bum, and then came back to the living room and cried to us. He said he couldn't believe what he had done. My stomach was feeling fucked, why's he telling me this, fuck you, you just hit my brother and I don't even like you.

I was putting up a fight in the home, didn't have the skills to know how to make this better for all of us though, so my violent rages were the side effect of confusion. A confrontational teenager, I would challenge my mum. The violence felt like safety. There was always calm in the flat after a big night of fighting. When I screamed at mum, Simon wanted to be her White Knight: he was as lost in this dynamic as the rest of us. He pinned my arms against the bookcase one time; I don't know why as I never hit my mum. He would hold me, restrained so she could hit me. I was raging, fighting with all I had while he continued to restrain me in place. Now it was two on one, what the fuck is this.?!

A few hours later he would come into my room crying, not understanding what he had done and would ask for forgiveness. I hated him. No you can't have my love or forgiveness. I would cry until my eyes were so puffy I could barely see on the top of my bunk bed, wondering how I could get out of this life.

I was 13 the first time I tried to take my own life. It all felt too much. I had read about suicide in Just 17 magazine, and was like yeah, I can do this. I took four Nurofen alone in my room. I know four can't harm me now, but to my teenage mind I believed it could. I just wanted it all to end but I panicked, thought of my siblings being left alone and the pain they would have to go through. The walls closing in, I went and told my mum and Simon what I had done. He took me to the toilet got me to drink five litres of water and then told me to put my fingers down my throat to make myself sick. I remember being on the toilet floor with him, thinking I was fighting for my life and wishing I had the guts to get out.

I would test my mum and I would test Simon: maybe I was wondering how far it would go. The violence escalated in the house as things among us all slipped out of control and our mum lost sight of who she was. The fights with Mum would get real bad, especially as I started to menstruate. She screamed that I needed a shag to sort me out, that it would stop my moods, like er how is sex gonna help a child? This twisted reality was manifesting madness in all of us. I would lash out at her with my words, calling her a fucking slag, a bitch, saying I didn't choose to be born. Simon would drag me to my room. Knocking me to the ground, he would sit across my waist, pinning me to the floor. At times he would leave my arms free and I would scratch and bite him. His upper arms were covered in scars from where I would fight him.

The aftermath was confusing. I would ask myself why I always had to be so naughty. I would drag my nails across my arms and bang my head on the wall, wanting to knock some sense into myself. I kept visualising suicide, 'cause this prison sentence did not have an end date. I had fantasies of being an actress one day, getting to nourish my talents, and this tiny glimmer of light saw me through. I would say to myself, just wait till you have your own life and the opportunity to be who you know you can be. This was all that kept me going. I wanted to know what I could create as an adult: I would give it a little time and if that didn't work then I would be checking out of this hell.

I screamed at Simon: YOU'RE NOT MY DAD. He would get enraged and drag me to my room by my hair and throw me against the wood table, my head smashed off the side. He then climbed on top of me again, restraining my arms. I was blank. All I could see was white in front of my eyes, every part of my being was raging, screaming into nothingness, physically in contact with him yet alone with my feelings of injustice. They had started to lock me in my room by tying the back of the door with a scarf to the bookshelf.

One time I had had enough, my rebel spirit blazing strong, I pulled and pulled at the door in my room. The door came clean off its hinges at the top and split the rest of the way down. The bookshelf fell down. The house was in a mess, which of course got me into greater trouble but I was surprised at my strength. I was free for another beating, and then would be ignored for days, no love yous, no way to make it better, no way out of the hole I had dug for myself. The door was left broken for as long as I could remember, split down the middle. I don't think the council fixes intentional damage.

Simon would feel bad after our fights and would sometimes buy me clothes, leaving gifts on my pillow in my room, or trying to be close to me. Why was I gonna be close to a man I didn't feel pure intentions from?

The last fight we had, I was taunting him. 'What you gonna do?' He was telling me off for my behaviour; Mum was out somewhere. My brother and I were doing it together like a game, come on then what you gonna do? We can do what we like our mum ain't here and you can't do a thing to us.

He kicked off at my brother, pinning him down then he got at me by the bookcase in the living room. He slapped me clean in the face just as my mum's friend Alex came into the room. I ran out of the house into the cold. I might as well have been running on a running machine 'cause where was I running to? I was 14 and didn't have anywhere to go, there was nowhere to run, no space to run to from the madness. The familiar feeling of tears burning, my body aching inside, the feeling of helplessness as I went to the estate, an unfriendly great mass of blocks that offered more bullies and no protection.

Alex had seen the reality of our home life. He brought me and my brother to McDonald's and we had hot chips, which was a real treat for us, then he took us home and we felt safe for that evening. Alex was horrified at what had gone on and had stern words with my mother that Simon had to leave as violence against her children was wrong on so many levels. Her twisted view of the world couldn't see that but she wanted to impress her friends so she was backed into a corner.

I wouldn't talk to Simon. I was done. He left an apology on my pillow, but I was so done with this game. It was not the way it should be. He was my mum's partner; the notes never gave me a good feeling.

Mum finished with him as she was outvoted by the other men in her life who stood up for us. I would try and talk of the stuff that Simon had done but I was told I was a liar by the woman who would spent her whole life talking about abuse. Ours weren't seen, only hers had relevance in that flat. Unheard feelings of injustice was like a t-shirt for my 15 year old self, the clothing I wore in this twisted existence. Years later, after the family broke down and everyone knew the truth of how bad it had got in our home, Mum's friends apologised to me for not believing what I had said. I had spent years with the burden of really believing that all that had happened at home was my fault. A vision of self built on a swamp that swallows all you believe to be true; the fight or flight mode confused like a bird without its homing instinct.

Hip Hop

I've got guts, like I say I'm gonna do something then I have to step into alignment with what I have just created for myself. This has been my experience with running events. I always had this feeling that I wanted to run an all-female hip-hop event from like around being 24 years old. It was a mad feeling; I was obsessed with female rappers since forever. I dunno why they're called female rappers as they are rappers that just happen to have vaginas, but hey, going with society and all that.

Ever since I first started to get the burn for the mic, a pull of fate to the world of hip-hop, I was in crowded rooms full to the brim with dudes, a couple of girls floating about but it was mainly a boys thing. Lyric Pad, a night in Camden used to encourage the girls a lot, which was awesome. I would stand on the stage during the cypher, with like ten men waiting to spray some bars and there is me, some mad colourful hippy waiting to get the chance to share my lyrics. I'd grab it when my turn came and spit for under a minute before the mic was grabbed away for the next person. I used to hit up these clubs on my own, and it was brutal in the front, the crowd pushing you 'cause the event is so rammed and the stage is small. How did I put myself in those spaces, a little white girl dropping knowledge on the beat?

I was starting to accept my sexuality, starting to want to express more of myself and I felt that an all-girl hip-hop night would be slamming; it was one of the main reasons I had started to work at the Candy Bar in Soho, but I was too scared to make it happen. One night, after a shift, I was in the back office with Kim Lucas, the woman who set up the Candy Bar, and Naj, the manager. I shared my idea of an all-female hip-hop event. Kim got out her diary and put in my first date: I would be paid a fixed fee each week to run the show. I had to book the acts, the DJs, and this was my chance on the mic – to be fully in this scene. I was bricking it, I had never run a show before and in three weeks' time I had to fully make this happen.

It was a free entry event as it was on a Sunday night right in the heart of Soho. The first night was rammed – super rammed – queue-around-the block packed, MC's gathered (the female kind) and girls smashed out the decks. It was a success and I was so, so happy. The dark basement of the Candy Bar was full to the brim, we played hip-hop, RnB, and bashment and finished off with a storming drum 'n' bass set. I think we were so buzzin' that my sister dropped a few of my bars on the mic. The energy was inspiring. The night had been a success, and it was incredible to see something in my head realised like that; to dive into unknown waters and swim like an Olympic athlete.

*****

The following week was good, but by the third week it was

dead and we didn't open up downstairs. Out of that first trial of the idea though, Lick It was born, a regular weekly night celebrating female talent, I used the Candy Bar as a woman's space instead of focussing on it as a gay female space, 'cause there weren't that many spaces for women to perform and get good in front of an audience. Most open mics were male-dominated or would have lots of singers. The night was for female performers to take to the stage invited onto it by me. We had acoustic events with poetry and hip hop events with all female line ups.

The third Sunday of every month was an all-female hip-hop line-up, with Lady Essie on Decks, Mad X on the mic, myself and Pariz I repping, plus nuff other girls that came through, including Kate Tempest, who set the mic alight one evening. There would be seven girls in a circle, passing the mic; a cypher in the underground bar. It's a lot more civilised when girls pass the mic. The all-girl hip-hop night weren't always rammed; the acoustic events proved to be a lot more popular. I had to book all the artists a month in advance to make sure we could get the flyers done in time.

I didn't have a contract on my phone then 'cause I was always living from place to place. I had some Nokia credits on my phone though, if I used £5 in a week that would give me 60 minutes of call time and unlimited texts to book the shows, so I was rationing the mins to get a full line-up each month, plus MySpace was poppin' back then so I maintained connections on that platform.

A promoter by default, the nights fluctuated. I started regularly running the event with Caz Coronel who had just started to DJ. We had a run of about six months where we were fully rammed, then it started to trail off. I was getting into cocaine at the time. I had been at Candy Bar just under three years and I had tried to stay away from Coke and stick to Mandy, but I wanted to know what all the fuss was and I started to use. I would turn up to run the event still high from the night before without going to sleep. I must have been using until 12pm the next day. I would wash, grab some more stuff on my way to work and carry on. No one at work cared 'cause everyone was getting mashed, it didn't matter that I turned up to work like that; I still got paid.

In the end, the venue got bought and we lost our jobs. The end of an era was upon us and the Candy Bar closed down soon after.

The whole experience had turned me off doing events. We had had success but it didn't grow, it didn't move to the next level. I was so done, but then I met Carina Wann at a burlesque event I dropped a poem at. She was involved with the Russian Bar as well as the Hobby Horse on Kingsland Road. She persistently e-mailed me for a year to have a conversation about running an event. I finally showed up one November in 2000 to the Hobby Horse – it was an old pub with lots of character. As Carina finished up her previous meeting I was being hit with inspiration; I was thinking how about an event where we challenged each other as poets. Instead of it being a slam it could be a space to share new pieces: so instead of always putting out to an audience our known crowd-pleasers, a challenge could be set for the poets that they had to perform on the night.

This idea became Lyrically Challenged. There was an open mic to warm up then it went straight into the challenges. The first event was half-ish full and we had some dope poets Tim Clair, Michelle Madsen, Dean Atta and more. I got paid and used the money to buy some coke and alcohol. I got mashed with my mates that night, the poets went home.

I did one more event in the snow at the Hobby Horse, but Carina Wan left and I was offered a bar split instead of a straight fee, without this even being discussed, so I was ready to leave. Eleanor Wilson and Planet Man had come out in the thick snow to see the show and I was offered a new residency at Passing Clouds – a magical porthole for the creative; a hive for the creatives who buzz about the space. It was a legally run club focussed on consciousness, community, free-man living and really very good live world music. And they were offering a better deal and more support than I had at Hobby Horse.
It was my job to book two artists and set up the event for the evening, putting out the chairs, setting up the stage and making sure the vibe was good. It was free entry for a while. A few people would come, like around 20 to 30 people, yet we persisted. Eleanor would hold regular meetings with me for a few hours to really look at how to develop the event, how to get more people into the door. I was used to bumbling by and pretending to myself I was reaching my potential. Eleanor had eyes and a vision for my life that I was blind to.

The event steadily started to grow into a community but then, six months into running the event, my mum passed away, and I didn't care too much any more about being an artist; the pain was so deep and all I saw for my future was a foggy haze of grief. I was consumed by the emotions and all my writing was from a heart broken into a million pieces.

I still did the events though. We started to attract a crowd that had been going through similar life situations: one young man shared his story of childhood abuse – he was a striking man who you never would have thought had been raped as a child. It became a space for realness, a space where the open mic was full of content from the heart minus the ego. We were starting to get rammed and the first birthday bash was packed solid. I had started to pay all the artists who performed and DJ Shorty came and joined the team. It took me a while to understand the importance of paying artists, how much artists are struggling to get by with their art.

Making money from the door and offering everyone a split made it pressured, but the pressure created heat and now we were on fire. The events were slamming. Alia joined the team with so many innovative ideas, involving graffiti art. I always felt so restricted by money, there was so much I didn't believe I could make happen before, being part of a team I was inspired and started to run a slick event. Sonority my good friend and local poet joined the team as well as Connie Bel a local artist connected to the Passing Clouds community, and Sonny Green a young 17 year old rapper from South End became a resident poet. Lots of the lesbian community came through, still connected from the Soho days when I worked at Candy Bar and MC'd at Heaven.

Eleanor Wilson, the founder of Passing Clouds, sat me down and said she could see me running two-floor hip-hop events there at Passing Clouds. She always beamed like a sun onto my shadows. I couldn't quite embrace her light – my life had been in winter for so long that I didn't fully believe in the sun. I moved into spring though, the glimmers of light started to pierce my being and I could see glimpses of Eleanor's vision. The event was getting so busy every Tuesday that we had to make a Friday night happen. The venue was booked and I was ready to take the reins. I had booked the upstairs acts as well as the downstairs act minus one BIG act. With the help of Eleanor and Alia, we drew up the line up. I wanted to book Akala with a live band for the event: his energy was the energy I was most connecting with especially after the 'Find No Enemy' video. His energy is revolutionary and stood in firm alignment with Lyrically Challenged. He was the perfect artist for us to grow with. We had Floetic Lara, Lady MC booked for the downstairs and we had some incredible acts for upstairs. The time was drawing close: I hadn't even really promoted yet and I was close to giving up on Akala as it didn't seem like it was going to happen. Sitting in my living room feeling defeated, I spoke to one of my best friends, Sacha, and was just about to look for a replacement, but Sacha knew his manager and was like, 'Girl, you really quittin'?' She sent an e-mail and by the end of the night we were on. It was such a blessing. We booked a super dope live band that learnt all his tunes. Vibes.

I had been on a detox since the beginning of January, it was our second birthday party and it was looking good: third week of February. As I chanted I visualised the building as a lighthouse and visualised the light beaming out into the surrounding area with everyone who visited the event receiving the light and bringing it back to their homes and communities. I liaised with the artists, wrote the running order on the night of the event and I hosted the entire event from 8pm–3am, including the cypher upstairs and downstairs, all while taking care of artists' payments and the flow of the evening. Nothing can beat the feeling of standing inside of my dream as a reality, not a knickerbocker glory when you're a kid, not sex with the buffest girl: it is the realisation that we are limitless, that I am limitless in that moment.

My heart was pounding hard before the event started, it felt like my chest would burst. I was sweating out in the rooms –

the spaces looked so big, I had wondered how we would fill the space. Seeing everyone turn up the anxiety faded in to a rose garden of magic and it smelled sweet out here. The event was one-in, one-out from 9pm, totally rammed through and through; friends couldn't even get in.

Inside my meditation in real time, the chants echoed through the universe. I was nervous through the whole thing and didn't enjoy much of it. All the acts absolutely slammed the event, Akala was amazing, he had the place jumping and the band played perfectly; Floetic Lara and Lady MC brought it as they always do. What an event.

When we were done for the night I felt like I deserved a 'treat' so had a bottle of rum and a gram of MDMA at 4am, I dunno why that felt like it was a good idea. I slept through to the next night then ended up raving for three days straight. My tummy was so fucked after I couldn't get out of bed.

I had my first ever Buddhist course that weekend. I couldn't chant, I didn't move from my bed for a week. I didn't even understand my addiction then, I thought heavy drinking and doing drugs was normal 'cause me and all my mates did it. Alone at home in my darkness, my blanket to life, not moving, I didn't have any positive visions in that moment. I would think of slitting my wrists, my head going crazy, just wanting to end that feeling while also wanting to get moving at the same time.

I would get back up though, and Lyrically Challenged was my push forward – there weren't much else: Buddhism and hip-hop were my lifelines in those moments.

The success of the show led to us running a Friday night slot at The Secret Garden Party with OneTaste a pioneering event in London which provided a space and a stage for many very well established artists to hone their craft: we had Kate

Tempest as the headline, Sonny Green, Kwake and Con, Caxton Press and ourselves the LC Collective: I had made a collective with my closest girls, Shay D, Emma Prior, Sirena Reynolds, Sonority and myself. We became an all-female hip-hop group with DJ Shorty to rep for the boys on the decks. We had our first set at the festival warming up for Kate, so the tent was rammed. We slammed our first packed show. It was dope, the crowd was 300-strong. Nothing can beat the feeling of the mic in hand, connecting to the crowd, feeling the crowd with you as you spit your bars, sharing a deeper part of yourself. To connect with a crew of girls rapping together on stage and to smash it was so awesome. the rhythm of unity we had created felt like a bubble bath hot and warm after a day out in the cold, warm and healing.

Kate had it packed out the door, Caxton Press went on after. They were heavyweight but it was my error in the running order: I should have put them before Kate. I under estimated how big her following had got. The gig was so live, electric bass beats bouncing off the speakers, the crowd jumping in time to the beats and repeating the chrous. Another slammed event, and now we had a crew – the LC Collective, our all-female hip-hop group.

Next big event was an all-female line-up at Passing Clouds for the night: hip-hop with girls headlining. I gathered all my main girls for this gig, Belle Humble, Lena Cullen, DJ Baby Blu, the graffiti girls outside from Girls On Top crew, myself and the girls with Shay D hosting a cypher upstairs. I literally went to every single party I was invited to promoting this show, sharing the flyers with as many people as I could. The overheads for the gig were at £2,000 and here I was penniless. If the gig fucked up I was broke and owing so many acts dough. I home visited every artists that was on the bill, personally sharing the vision of the event with each one of them, aligning the energies so we were all excited and building the event as a team.

I spent hours at home inboxing people about the event on Facebook until I would get banned from posting to inboxes, until I got banned from sending tweets, putting flyers in all the shops, a one-woman mission. Shay was getting really involved at this point; she was putting in the same energy as me: we were forming a partnership without me realising it. We were hip-hop sisters whose passion burned to the same flame and now we were blazing a trail in London with a platform for conscious rap.

Such a mix of people turned out for the event, from rude boys to hippies to Lesbians – there were nuff lesbians at this event. It was a London melting pot of ethnicity, bouncing to the bass lines and vibing to the beats. We became a family, with love, we tore down the gender norms and passed the mic to the boys who perfectly stepped into the space we created with conscious bars on the beats. Then the girls took the mic back and tore it up. Creating equality through the love of music – non-intentional revolutionary moves 'cause music has that magic pull that has the power to transform the world. Hip-hop has always been about the voice of the oppressed people; it's always been a way to shout out from the rubble society creates for many people and to shatter the binds that hold us back and use them as a platform for growth.

The event was a success – another success –and it was such a crazy feeling to fully understand the power of unity, to watch an event grow from 20 people in a pub to 500, celebrating women in hip-hop with the men by our sides, an equal part in this movement. I went home with money in my pocket, sober and woke with £500 profit for the first time. I went and bought myself some new boots. I had given everyone a bonus, including Shay D, 'cause she had smashed it helping with the event. In the crowd watching some acts during the night, I asked Shay if she would like to run the event with me; we may as well share it all.

We then got a Friday night residency at Passing Clouds as the Tuesdays were too busy. It was time to grow. We started to work smarter, and now I had finally given up drinking I attracted new friends – Shay had always been sober. We shared everything, all the highs and the lows, the times where we worked our asses off all month to barely breaking even, building all the contacts in the hip-hop world. At first everyone wanted to charge top rate cause Lyrically Challenged didn't yet have the rating to secure big acts at mate's rates. We were in an unknown world, like a computer game where you're a character that is dropped somewhere and you've got nothing; you have to earn swords to cut through the jungle and you gotta earn shields to protect you when you're attacked: we were naked in this new world of promotion.

Second Time Getting Nicked

It was New Years' Eve, the turn of the millennium. London was hype – well the whole world was hype. It was the turning of a time. Prince's record, '1999' was playing out of all the shops everywhere, plus there was lots of fear propaganda about the end of the world coming. I didn't care much, I smoked spliffs for breakfast and wore depression as my attire: 18 and tired of life.

I was spending the day and evening with a best mate, Sally: it was her birthday on New Year's Day, so we were gonna celebrate, but she couldn't get a babysitter for her daughter. We fell asleep then woke in the morning to half a bottle of Bacardi. Her sister had taken her daughter, so we started the millennium with a drink. We bought some more drink, got dressed, bunned a couple of joints. I was entering the year 2000 drunk and high looking for trouble.

We rode the underground, jumping up and down, sitting in different seats. Sally was shining an infra-red light at people and bugging them out. One woman was genuinely smiling at me in a loving way: I threw a bottle of water all over her. We thought this was so funny, cracking up all the way through the tunnels. I was pouring my discomfort all over passengers: it felt like fun in that moment, sharing my suffering with destruction.

Sally had been in care most her life – as had most my mates. We were the girls without stable families. We decided to go to Sally's old children's home, knocked the door and the staff let us in. We were billing spliffs in the toilet of the home then smoking out the back, with spirits in our coke cans. We thought we were so undercover but it was bait, dunno how the staff put up with us. The house was nice and in a posh area, Crouch End sides. Loads of rich houses lined the roads and there was this one house where kids with no parents to support them lived together with staff. They knew we were fucked but what can you do with two young women who are fucked?

We left in the darkness of the night, knocking on random people's doors, asking them for help to open our bottles of wine. We backed a bottle then smashed it in half, putting it in Sally's jacket for protection 'cause anything could happen. We started to break off car wing-mirrors with our arms, lifting up the arm then slamming it down on the wing-mirror, which knocked it clean off. It seemed like fun at the time. A couple of curtain twitchers watched out of their windows. We tried to run past and hide. Some woman had said she'd called the police. We saw them coming and ran, but we had actually doubled back on ourselves and landed right in front of the police car. We knew they were coming for us.

I told Sally to hold tight as she hadn't noticed them. I threw a wing mirror into the bush. They asked, 'Have you been breaking wing mirrors?' I said no, even though they had seen me throw the Mercedes wing-mirror I had just broken into the bush right in front of them. The coppers pulled the mirror from the bush, found the bottle in Sally's jacket but didn't tell us off for the drink; they threw it in the bush.

The cuffs on and we were in the back of the car. This being my second time being arrested, I knew the drill and didn't go into panic mode. I was prepared to go through the motions. We were too drunk to be questioned so it was dry-out in the cell for the night. Whitewashed walls with graffiti carved into the paint from other bored prisoners. There was a bright white light which didn't get turned off even for the night and a blue scratchy blanket that sticks to your clothes but I didn't care in that moment – I was just tryna sleep.

Sally was in the cell next to me, screaming my name, SHAUNA SHAUNA SHAUNA SHAUNA. I could hear her crying. I didn't answer her even though everything inside of me wanted to comfort her. I knew it weren't leading anywhere good for us. I had to concentrate on getting myself through the night. The bed was spinning a 1,000 miles an hour, or was that my head? Luckily there was a toilet in my cell 'cause I was puking my guts out every 20 minutes. I wished I could turn the light off but when you have committed a crime you know that there aren't any allowances. In the morning, they opened the flaps of our cells and let us talk. Sally said she didn't know I was there, and I lied and said, 'Neither did I,' in a convincing tone. The truth didn't deserve a space in that moment.

We got moved to another station taken in the back of a meat wagon, locked in a cage, sitting on tiny benches at the back of a van. Sally was given an envelope to puke in. Here we were in this tiny space, her throwing up next to me, gross. The van was stinking out and my stomach was still churning from a night of being sick myself.

Another four hours in the cells, fingerprints taken, all my tattoos and piercing written down; they even took my DNA. It felt like forever in the cell this time, longer than the night before. The locked door didn't scare me so much now, but the helpless feeling of not being able to leave when you want to is crushing, a feeling of falling without ever being caught.

I got taken to the interview room and declined a solicitor 'cause I knew they wouldn't do much since it was just a couple of wing mirrors. It felt like being in an episode of The Bill when they pressed the tape on and off and put the cassettes into cases. I didn't care to be represented, having no love for myself and no love for my life. There weren't any consequences that could scare me.

After what felt like a lifetime we got out and sparked a fat spliff from the hash they had failed to find on us. Standing at the top of the hill, we got intoxicated again. All the charges were dropped as I knew they would be. I did learn a lesson though, and was always a lot more cautious of getting nicked again in the future.

How Far Would You Go For Love?

You gave birth to me, love flowed unconditionally, the umbilical cord attached spiritually, life we shared, pain destruction, yet love was there.

You, from Ireland ravaged from abuse, left alone on the cobbled streets for the fiends to use, barely older than two, I can't imagine what you've been through but the pain you carried I carried it too.

A mum so confused, 4 children no help, what to do but drink, lose the soul, mind eyes blind, can't think, children lost to the heart just sink, deeper. The downward spiral was chosen, lost in despair alone, then social services involved so the children are stolen.

Tried to help you, yet your warped view saw that as destruction too, can't help if you can't help you.

I had so much love, took abuse, tried to save you with my love, got knocked back, beaten, emotionally abused, pushed and shoved yet I would go back for more. Believed our relationship could survive cause I wanted a mother's love.

One day I walked away from the pain put a lock on my heart not to be opened again, given up on this love, allow this cycle, bored of the game looking for change. Out of sight out of mind then I'm free from the pain. That was a lie and I knew it but I needed the illusion to stop me going insane.

A family tattered and confused no sunshine always rain, closed my mind when I heard your name. As if I didn't hear it and you didn't exist, now so I'm free once again. Sibling love saw us through, fed each other love like food, tryna heal the wounds yet it didn't feel right without you being part of the love too.

Birthdays and Christmas I'd get pissed, lost in the mist to escape the loneliness. We were all apart, like at different corners of the world, pull the blanket over my head then curl. Laying in the foetal position, the comfort it brings, yet ours was tainted so I existed in the dream.

The anger and rage turned into a dull grey space, years go by and I hoped to find a way to love and accept you the way you are, no judgment just the purity of an open heart. I never reached that place while you were alive and the lesson leaves a bitter aftertaste.

You left this world with your heart broken, literally broken, alone. Arteries blocked choking, no air the soul left your body on the bed, days gone by 'til someone found you there.

I was shocked in despair, been expecting that call for years yet it was still a surprise to hear, to hear that you died, left us behind, tears flowed from my soul though my eyes.

I had missed you for years yet blanked the feeling so well that when you died the illusion died and the emotions appeared. I realized how much I love you, felt for all the madness you had been through. You didn't have much of a chance for the start and tried your best to raise four children alone in Camden on an estate torn apart.

The funeral was such a beautiful goodbye…. Your favourite songs, the true rebel spirit from you was alive, your whole family and friends by our side, the powerful healing your departure provides! Was a magical day your soul dancing with pride.

In meditation we spoke, said sorry to each other, a true blessing between daughter and mother. I heard you loud and clear not like a ghost to fear a true connection that I hadn't felt for years.

Your ashes came back to the family home, we put a candle on top, lit it, at family gatherings it danced and we knew we weren't alone, first Christmas in years the whole family united, you on the mantelpiece the flame dancing your presence invited.

Free from your body and pain filled memories, your soul danced happily, then it was time to take you home back over the Irish sea with your ancestors to rest peacefully,

On the train to the airport a mother and daughter sat in front of me, daughter's head on the mother's shoulder I could have felt jealous but I held my rucksack that holds your ashes tightly, our relationship troublesome to say the least yet here I was carrying your ashes honouring your wishes completely

You made peace with your home and your family, we got to our destination, a whole tribe of us sending you off on your last goodbyes, I said a few words tried to hold back the tears forming in my eyes, we spoke of unity and the love that your death survives

Into the river you loved as a child, your ashes spread at the bottom of the lake, we saved a few to put on your ancestors grave, I felt light, the sun shone, what a perfect day, you free in the picturesque mountains, free from the death trap known as Camden.

I have been through such a journey with this love, I have learned so much, and miss you so it's been more than tough, feels crazy to miss you cause we had no contact while you were here, writing this eyes full of tears, I love and appreciate all you gave, now you rest peacefully so, dancing on the clouds, free, love you forever mummy

UK Gold

Every year I try to find a way to deal with the anniversary of my mum's passing, running an event, not getting fucked up on drink or drugs and this year we went to Ireland to visit her ashes. It was a powerful trip. On the Friday when we got back to London we were meeting with the family for dinner, I got a group message about a Uk Gold show that needed a female rapper. I sent a demo of my work straight away and didn't hear anything back. Ended up having a big fight with my sister on the Friday at the family dinner and was like FUCK IT I will not have anyone call me names ever and I went back to my flat in Camden..

This triggered a deep depression. It hurt so much inside. I chanted, tried to work through the energy. I found a wrap of coke and opened it and was so close to sniffing the powder. Luckily the strong part of me threw it in the toilet 'cause them demons are strong in me — I gotta move myself out of the way. I sunk low, my heart was burning. If my phone rang I wouldn't answer, just watched the screen like a pretty light, wanting to communicate but being so stuck in my darkness, closed curtains and closed soul. On the Sunday I managed to get to a Buddhist meeting and a chant session then back home to my empty space.

I received a text from my friend that the UK Gold producers wanted to meet me the next day for a role in the drama the next morning. I woke the next morning and I was free from the pain. It had left me. The chanting was enough to lighten me up and I went for the audition. I was playing a 'rapper' in a halfway house with a fictional king who was changing up his PR to reach the Youth!

I arrived at a swanky building in the west end, went to a big room with glass tables and met the producers of the show, some middle-aged white guys who were very friendly. We got the script and a brief. I was to rewrite the lyrics and perform for them: I had 15 minutes to do this. I rewrote the bars with Grace Savage the Beat Boxer providing the beat. The producers came back in and we delivered with a powerful passionate energy.

The feedback was that the bars needed to be more 'street' but they loved the performance. I was so thankful for the bits of chanting I was able to fit in between my depression on the weekend before the audition 'cause I could lighten up and create. It showed me that all the good causes I have been making in my life were seeing me through, and that the deperession I suffer don't mean I'm a bad person, it's a symptom of PTSD. It also didnt' hold me back, as I was able to move through it just in time thankfully.

I stopped in a cafe on my way to a meeting. I had half an hour so I wrote a lyric full of slang words to make it sound more 'street' as the producers had asked. Then I rewrote the bars cause I don't use slang that much in my raps, being a white girl and all I don t think it suits my style. I sent it to them and nailed it.....YES YES YES. I still didn't feel good that me and my sister wasn't talking but I had to keep creating good fortune in my life and this role was made for me; telling a king he don't get how it is for us on the streets in a rap to an audience of millions. I had to make that happen. Fuck, fighting depression and myself to hear the light within the truth. I have to know how much I can do with my gifts.

The day came for the shoot, I couldn't believe it, I was so excited. I had a 10am call time. enough time to stretch and go for a run before the shoot. I got picked up by a private driver in a blacked out Mercedes 'cause they're used to driving famous people about. Well here was my taste of a world I used to fantasise about being part of from my bunk bed in my flat in Camden. I was inside my own vision so many years later at 35, an eyeblink of success. It was a bit boring in the car, I scrolled through FaceCrack; I wish I could say it was more glamourous. I arrived at a car park in High Wycombe. There were trailers, it was dark and grey and rainy. I was put on a bus with lots of other people – I was unsure of who was who, and felt a little lost. Then I was called for make-up and apologised to 'cause I didn't have my own trailer for the day. I was brought to make-up and the woman applied heavy eye shadow and left behind the foundation. I had a couple of monster spots so got that sorted. Everyone was so lovely, very friendly.

I was brought to the crew bus, which had tables like a cafe and a TV playing. I was told that my clothes were perfect for the role so there wasn't a need to visit wardrobe. I was sitting in full make-up in a bus alone and it was chapping. I was practising my lyrics while I was on the bus, like a crazy person chatting to myself. Grace Savage arrived at like 12.30pm: she had been stuck in a load of traffic. We caught up on the bus, cracked jokes and talk about the lesbian scene.

We got our lunch before the extras and it felt strange to see a bus full of hungry people who reached the set before we did sitting there cold while we grabbed our hot food and went off to our more chilled bus. We ate with the director and producer and talked spoken word and film. The divide bothered me but I was hungry and cold so I did enjoy the fact I got my food quickly, was happy I never became an extra. Even being the 'talent' for the show with our headshots in the production office there ain't a thing that is glamorous about hanging out in a car park in the pissing rain all day. I stood by cars with drops of rain falling on me, on the grey rubble concrete chatting my lyrics out loud. Dunno how I wrote them. I didn't edit so the flow was hard to catch and I had to invent a different kind of rhythm to fit a steady beat.

Finally we were taken to the set. We were driven in a Rolls Royce: now I was feeling the glamour – for a whole ten minutes in an eight hour day. We arrived at an old building that was used as the local youth club in real life. We played table tennis just like I do at work and we waited another couple of hours while getting our make-up constantly retouched as they filmed some other scenes. Our scene was the last scene of the day.

The guy who was playing the King of England was outside, arriving to the club as the extras waved him in with Union Jack flags. Once again I felt for the extras: they were outside freezing and we were inside the club – bored, but at least we were warm and dry, but I wasn't complaining that we got paid around ten times the amount they did.

It was time for our shot. It got lined up with three cameras pointing at us to get three angles at once. I was fully shitting myself and wondering if I could remember my lines and get the flow on point. And this whole situation was tripping me out to the maximum. I was on a stage in a youth club, I had been working in youth clubs for the past 15 years of my life, I'd dedicated all my life to speaking up for under privileged young people. I was playing a rapper – I am a rapper – who is in a half-way house just out of jail – I lived in a hostel for homeless people and that is where I started rapping. Then my role in my bars is to ask this king how he could step in here with his jewels: he didn't know what it was like out there for us. In the storyline this changes the king's perception on life and he wants to do more to help.

It was like everything that has been in my heart was magnified in this moment; all I had been through and had cared about was in the character I got to play in the show. The biggest audience I had ever reached would be connected to my deepest prayers. I was tripping out on how trippy this was then the director yelled action. I somehow remembered my bars, remembered to look at the king, who was watching us on this 'stage' in the youth club – and slammed it. We had to do a good few takes to get all the angles. I started cracking jokes, saying I'd waited all my life to make it, that I couldn't believe I was in High Wycombe. The director loved this and asked me to put it in to the next few takes. We managed to nail it and everyone clapped, it was like a real show.

We got to ride back to the base with the main actors who were playing the lead roles for the show. A whole day of waiting around to then bring the big energy and deliver on the spot. For it all to be over before it began, to be riding back with professional actors. It was all a lot for me to take in. I believe in my talent as a performer and I love feeling the highs of talent being recognised, but to see the extras not getting paid as much and working ten times harder I found hard. I had to play myself and my former self in one go: I was that girl I just played and I am the rapper that spat the bars.

We reached the car park, the actors were super lovely, taking pics and hitting us up on twitter. I said bye to Grace and got in my car to be dropped home. I was with one of the lovely actors who had just stared in Bridget Jones Diary, we started to talk about Buddhism. It turned out one of the other main actors in our show was also a Nichiren Buddhist: what are the odds of that? So much of this show was in synchronicity with my life. We connected with spiritual discussions all the way home, back to my Council Flat in Camden.

When I got home I had my study group with the girls I support at the local centre. The chanting grounded me and the study deepened my faith. What a trippy day, getting a month's wages in a few hours, speaking up for what I really believe in, set in a setting that has always and still does hold so much meaning to me. The deeper I go into my practise, the more I offer my life and my talents to Kosen Rufu (world peace), the more the universe responds. It cuts through all the stuff that just don't need to be there as I draw life force for the practice for peace, my life amplifies the opportunities that shine.

I need to keep transforming the poison of my life into medicine; my Karma into mission. Energy is energy, the negative can be used for positive and suddenly I am appearing in worlds I had only seen in my mind's eye, just by speaking from my heart. The deeper my faith goes, the more my life confirms that my faith is correct, that I can transform so much more than my mind can understand. I need to keep broadening my perspective through chanting and study, working through the pain and discomfort of a broken childhood growing up in poverty to being driven in Rolls Royce's. I'm not in this for the glamour even though it is comfortable. I am in this to say, hey things ain't right down here, down where the poor people are, it's fucked. That is exactly what my character said for the biggest show of my career so far. Life is next level: this is all next level. When I open my life to the infinite power of the universe I know we have the power to make the change: we are the change the world needs to see.

Hanwick

can't see the stars
when the blocks eat into the sky
the gutter washes away hope
no gold on these streets
dreams are built on rubble pathways
sirens the soundtrack in the concrete jungle
the pack in blue coats
cage the so-called wild beats

i grew up
on castle road
council estate no kings no thorns
wished dad was a Knight
he disappeared in dark rooms
chasing dragon's smoke
mum full of history, arts, music, poetry and magic
4 seeds violent rages her story was tragic
poverty mind state trappings
flats a maze no escapings
the streets the teacher
lessons at the top of the blocks
hopeless backdrop

chemical grade As
burned in a haze
criminal aspirations
jail bars to tombstones
graduation
pain blaneted into darkness
my dark skies are starless
15 suicide to leave my life
tried but
keep thinking of the siblings I would leave behind,

Don't give up the fight, Don't give up the fight, Don't give up the fight

the storms of this sea carried a ferocious rage
red hot tears burn my face
my bro's skitzo locked in a cage
ill fate
the boys on the estate, all suffered the same
gradually voices lead to insanity
they fed him pills thieves of humanity
mum housing demons
spirits screaming
younger bro n sis now victims in the system
if home's where the heart is my,
heart's scattered into fragments
maddened in sadness

Don't give up the fight, Don't give up the fight, Don't give up the fight

21 homeless in King's cross
hostel life costs
live with ladies of the night
work erodes their souls
they get junked out before the pain takes hold
determined to rise from my fall
divine timing aligned with my mentor
my angel
vision in a visionless space
encouraged talents
rapping and acting....

now it's big shows with bright lights
flying
mic in hand reaching dreams
build on quicksand of low self-esteem
haunted by shadows, karmic ghosts
dancing with spirits, highs can't beat the lows

don't give up the fight, Don't give up the fight, Don't give up the fight,
don't give up

how can I not give up, when everything that used to have meaning
means nothing,
and u don't give a fuck, Lost Mum

she begged for rehab
no funding
in a world where it's profits before people
a currency of evil
i kneeled and I prayed
mantras that's mystic
poison is my medicine
pain into mission

Don't give up the fight, Don't give up the fight, Don't give up the fight,

Don't give up

Cornwall

Cornwall

I had just turned 20 and I was waiting for my younger brother to go to his foster home. It was torturous, like waiting for food to cook, watching it intently then suddenly it's burnt beyond the edible stage and there ain't no other food or money. It felt like that but worse because no amount of food could ever feel like a brother or fill the space of feeling like a failure to one of the people I love most on the planet.

A few weeks before, a family friend had taken myself and my sister to Cornwall for a week, and we loved it. The sign on the pub was a ray of hope. I got a job as a chef's assistant for the Summer and I was gonna leave it all behind and start a new life. I didn't have many clothes or many belongings, less than a suitcase full. My younger brother left for his new home in East London with a cockney family who had loads of parrots and animals. I brought him to his new home, heartbroken again, then I got on the train leaving this fucked life in London.

I was going to Cornwall with no money, no idea of where I was going to sleep, didn't know any people. I didn't feel afraid, the emptiness inside was vast. I was searching for a light to guide me so I walked in the dark hoping Cornwall would provide the flame. I had a job, I held on to the good I could in this situation. On the train the tracks move London further and further into the distance until there were green blurs whizzing past on the side of the tracks, countryside.

I had a very shit little tent, which I pitched hoping to get away with not paying on the grounds of the campsite we had stayed on with our mum's mate. I managed to get one night's stay and got kicked off by a sexy boy. I kinda liked boys back then, and he was nice. I hid my suitcase and the tent in the bushes near to the little old English pub that was to be my workplace for the summer. I went into the pub to check in for my start date. I was to start the next day in the upstairs kitchen, working 8 to 12 hour days, many split shifts. I was down with that; I didn't have much else to do so a full time job suited me.

I had £5 in my pocket, my last bit of money as Sainsbury's had owed me holiday pay when I left. But they fucked me over. I hadn't been a very good staff member, always bunking off work with depression so I suppose it was Karma. I was penniless and didn't have anywhere to stay. I spent the day by the sea on the sandy shore with the never ending horizon in the distance, watching the waves roll in and roll back out again.

That night I couldn't think of how to get somewhere to stay. The summer light and warmth had gone for the day, leaving me with darkness and no shelter for the night. I pulled out my sleeping bag from the big bush I had hidden it in and tried to sleep outside in the bush for the night. I was terrified, every little noise sounded like thunder, my heart was pounding, and I tossed and turned all night. I didn't have any tears left, I just kept telling myself off for being so stupid and wondering why

I had got myself into this situation. It was the longest night in hell; I was imagining rats running across me, or getting dragged out of the bush and raped by a man. FUCK that weren't a good time. I promised myself that I would never sleep rough again: that would be it.

I had a cheque guarantee card and a cheque book. There was no money in my account but the guarantee card meant the bank would pay up no matter what. I had no feeling for consequences; I was homeless, alone in a new place. I had to make it work somehow, 'cause living in a bush weren't where I planned to end up. I found a campsite about a mile up the road, in a field with a shower block, £35 a week. It was as basic as it gets but quite beautiful, with a big hill opposite and nice people around, no parties or big families passing through. With my cheque book I got myself a better tent. This was going to be my home for the next six weeks. I also got a warmer sleeping bag and a couple of bits like a swimming costume; spending money I didn't actually have was working.

I set up my home for the summer. I had a very basic 3-man tent, one I could stand in. I made myself a bed on the floor but didn't have a pillow so used my clothes to rest my head. It was a tiny space but a space to escape the family trauma that haunted my spirit.

I would walk along the country lane to work then home again in the evening. At night I would burn a little bit of hash – I'd found a dealer almost as soon as I got there. I would smoke, open up my tent and look at the stars. There were so many on the clear nights, I felt like I was lying inside the galaxy. A couple of times in London I might catch a star here and there if I was lying on the roof of a block of flats, but here I became a part of the sky, every night conversing with the universe.

The stillness was soothing me, walking along the river to work in the mornings avoiding the main road, either way was safe but the river was prettier. I worked in a little kitchen upstairs on my own assisting the chef. I prepared all the side salads for the meals, the sandwiches and the puddings. It was quite a job, I would have to run up and down the stairs to collect the orders and to bring the plates. It was very physical but it was good for me. The chef was an alcoholic but a functioning one, not like a totally fucked drinker, she managed to manage both a kitchen and her life on the drink. The landlady was lovely, the kinda woman one would want as your mother or grandmother. Grey hair, slim frame, always well dressed and presented nicely with a smile that felt like home.

After my first week I had a meltdown, crying hysterically, the guilt pouring from every part of my being, the stress coming out. I was trying so hard to do my best to be a good person but giving up my younger brother and sister was eating into my soul. How could I be here without them? I had to get on with it. The boss supported me and wiped my tears with a tissue. I worked five days a week doing double shifts. After the lunch rush I would go to the sea, put on my bikini and disappear into the waves, my little paradise. I pretended I was a mermaid, swimming under the water for as long as I could, feeling Mother Nature hold me with her power, I was free. My illusionary world, no human chains: I was a fish and a princess of the ocean.

It was a solitary time. I did make friends with some of the other young people who worked at the pub. I hung out with them occasionally but never became part of their scene. Twins worked there, I wanted to tell them I was bisexual but I hadn't made my mind up about that yet so keep myself quiet. The boy hooked me up with hash and sometimes we smoked together

My bro came out to visit me as well as my mum's old friends – a couple and their daughter. It was good to have a car and to move about. My bro didn't want to go everywhere with them, and I didn't have the time to look after him full-time as I was at work so he had to do what was asked of him. He must have still been so angry with me for the whole fucked up situation. We went to paradise-like beaches, body-boarded in Newquay, had adventure walks; it was as healing as it could be at that time.

I was doing well for around five weeks. I was always on time for work, I was on point with all I needed to get done, but toward the end of my stay I felt old patterns returning. I went into town one morning when I should have been working and went into a pub for a drink, looking for friends. I met a boy. He was drinking alone, he had shaggy blonde hair and blue eyes, and was as willing to get fucked up as I was, so he would do. I had found some company for my misery, good-looking company, too, so it was all good. He was a wanderer just like me, no stability, no home. I had had a summer of sun and sand but I had lacked the sex and that boy would do; and he would follow me about to get some.

I brought him to the pub I worked in, we had another couple of drinks then walked up the country lane to my little campsite. I got him in the shower, then fucked him for a couple of days. He weren't a very good lover, didn't like giving head, or making sure that I came. He started to try and talk 'we' language in the morning, but I was not getting into 'we' with him. He disappeared a few days later, must have got nicked or something. I was happy he was on his way: I'd had my fill and now it was time to get on with it.

I tried to hold onto the happy life I had created in Cornwall, but as the time slipped away, and the reality of going back to London crept up on me I felt myself slipping away too. Yet another day I was meant to be working I ended up in the pub, caring for work, for routines, for anything was flowing through my fingers like tryna grasp at sand.

I spent the day drinking alone in a town I had never been to before and where I didn't know anyone. I sat with some men and asked where I could get some hash to smoke. I was taken to the top of the pub, people were raving up there, crushing up pills and snorting them. I was 20 years old, alone and wondering how the fuck I had got myself here.

The next day I went back to the mad pub, met up with some guys again who invited me back to a house party. I had a little Mickey Mouse purse with very little money in it but I didn't care much, I got into the car high and drunk with the guys. This guy's house was dark and smelly; a little party flat that was lacking love, dirty sofas, overflowing ashtrays with a half working TV on an old busted stand. There was a little stereo to play music. I drank, bunned weed, drank, popped pills and sniffed some speed. My head spinning I locked myself in the toilet, puking, then passed out on the floor. I woke to some boys kicking the door in. They carried me to the sofa. I woke the next morning and carried on smoking and drinking with the guy whose flat it was until I had no money left and it was time to go home.

I got one of the boys I knew from the pub to pick me up in his car, packed away my tent and belongings and drove off the site without paying my last week's rent. My heart was pounding as I left the site; the man who lived there had always been good to me, inviting me in for meals and treating me as family.

I couldn't think, nothing mattered. I hadn't eaten in days. Fuck life.

The boy took me to his place where they were having band practise. I drank a bit and smoked some more hash, the world spinning. I was ready to bunk the train back to London. When I got on the train, I tried to dodge the guard but he caught me, took me to the front and I cried my eyes out. I said I was 15 and had run away and I was tryna get back to London. He took my address and let me stay on the train. It was such a long journey back, my stomach doing flips all the way. There was a big woman with two burgers in front of her. I was so tempted to just take one from her. I ignored the hunger pangs. I had created this mess.

I smelled London before I saw it: the green countryside turned into a grey blur, and then I arrived in Paddington. I begged a stranger for 20p then I called Janx, this rasta man I used to get drunk with. He came and got me. I moved into his place with his girlfriend. This was the start of the downward spiral: lost, alone and broken.

Grandad

Everyone has a different version of him. I don't connect to my mum's version of the violent man she described. The last time I saw him was in the summer just gone: he was a frail old man, lying down in his chair as he couldn't walk much those days at 94 years of age. He remembered me and said, 'Shauna, get here now and say hello, you look just like your mother.'

I try not to feel insulted, because his memory of her is full of love and I suppose he is extending that love to me in his own way. My memory of her is so tainted with pain and hate, but I let his love heal some of my pain.

He calls my sister and says, 'I don't remember you as much, but let's have a look at ye.' My nieces meet their great-grandfather in the Dublin Suburbs for the first time. At 5 and 9 years of age they're afraid of old age; they'd not seen a person that old before. It brought back memories of grandad's sister, Great Aunty Bridie, who was married to Kieron. Kieron had massive hairy lumps on his hands and we used to crack up into laughter when any one of my siblings had to sit next to him or on his lap; so I got where my nieces were at.

I call my Grandad a stallion: he married twice and had 14 children in his lifetime. He ran a business, started off with a wheelbarrow and a spade and grew it into a hardware shop. A pitbull; a warrior; a man of God. My strongest memory was his eyebrows: they spoke with him, so furry, so big, so thick with hairs that ran wild across his forehead. They moved to the rhythm of his stories and he was a good storyteller.

He would call us into his room – all the cousins, there were around eight of us, all young at the same time – and we would pile onto his bed, with the statues of Jesus and Mary on the dressers. It was kinda scary, like God was watching us. He would tell us stories of animal kingdoms that would always inevitably lead to a story connected to the bible. Then the rosary would come out, we would kneel on the cold floor. It was cold in the flat above his shop in the winter, the beads looked so massive and it felt like forever to get through them. The rosary was ten little beads, which were our fathers, and the big bead, which was hail Mary. This went on for like an hour. I was always tryna impress my grandad so I would recite the rosary to the best of my ability.

One night I got back from being out with the family and Grandad said, 'Go put on one of ye Aunty's dresses now'. My aunty was only five years older than me. I put on one of her old dresses, a blue and grey-checked dress. He said he was taking me out. I felt so special: my siblings weren't invited; this must mean that I'm his favourite. In my mind I was inventing all kinds of scenarios, burger joints, funfairs and other fun places that children like to go, just me and my grandad. But that wasn't the reality: he brought me to the house of two old ladies where we said the rosary for hours on our knees. I got some biscuits and a can of Fanta after the prayers; the sugar was a welcomed treat as we weren't allowed much sugar at our mum's, so I suppose some kinda treat happened.

I wanted to be a good Catholic: I was super excited to go to mass. Myself and my cousin, who was the same age as me, (we were round 9 years old) got up at 5am for 6am mass with grandad. It was a small church but looked huge to my 9-year-old self. Jesus hung from crosses with blood dripping from the marks where the nails hit his hands. Stained glass illuminated the church with the light streaming through the colours. We said mass for what felt like forever. I had pink rosary beads and I knelt for Christ. They went to get the bread and the wine but I weren't allowed to go 'cause I never had a communion. I felt like that was well out of order: I had said all the prayers and yet I weren't invited to break bread with the rest of the people. It felt like a lifetime while they went up and collected the communion from the priest. I donated two pence to the collection box: it was all I had in my pocket. I remember feeling kinda hard done by after the efforts I had made.

*****

My memories are in snippets of this man and so much is connected to his religious beliefs. Maybe that's where I get my strong faith from and committed practice. We went to Ireland after our family had fallen apart, after our mum had lost custody of her children. We were having an emergency meeting to see how we could move forward 'cause here were four children without parents – so we reached out to the ones we didn't know.

Grandad spoke right at the very end and said, 'No one has

spoken about love.' I remember thinking, 'Yes, why has no one spoken about love?' Then he said, 'the love of God.' Of course he did. How disconnected to the moment, but I guess that's how he connected to the moment. He was offering what he had. I didnt know how to connect God to the tragedy of that situation.

Grandad was of a different generation to us and I suppose he did the best he could with what he had. When Mum passed away we hadn't seen him for maybe ten years or so. He came back to London, lucky thing he could still walk and had some strength. Mum had made peace with him at that point in her life; I was trying to honour the place she had got to by welcoming the same into my life. The whole family arrived in London to honour the life of our mum; we met with everyone up in Golders Green. They were all staying close to the crematorium. We had dinner in a run-down pub and I sat with Grandad.

We followed my mum in a car on the way to the service. It was such a moving service. Towards the end Grandad got up and asked to say the rosary. He knelt and cried, his voice shaking as he said out loud his special prayers, blessing the passing of his precious daughter. The strength that shone through the cracks in his words moved the church to tears as we joined him in this moment of sadness, connected as a family to a broken woman who had lost her way.

This last time I saw Granddad he was 94, lying in his chair. He got up this time to greet us, joined us in the kitchen, a small round table, and food was brought out. It was ham cheese and bread: I'm vegan but was hungry so I got on with eating what had been put in front of me. Grandad didn't say much. He opened and closed his mouth with a little saliva falling from his lips. Everyone put lumps of butter on the bread the Irish way: as a child I never understood how that could taste nice and why the butter was so thick on the bread.

His mind was still sharp as a razor. We were in the garden sipping tea, he joined us just at the front by the patio. I'm told that this was a good day for him. Everyone was talking of leaving and he snapped suddenly to the conversation; his body weak but his mind still connected. He says, 'They're talking of leaving.' I was surprised to see him clock onto the conversation. That was to be the last time I saw him, and my heart sings that I get to remember him as this old sweet man, not as the violent man that had been described to me by my mother. I felt his violence through the hands and fists of my mother, her rage inherited from him; we felt the wrath, a second generation of Irish beatings.

Israel

It had been years since I had travelled anywhere, and six months into my new alcohol-free life. I was ready to fly the nest and to get out of town. I didn't yet have the money to go, so my best friend Emma had fronted it all for me, including the flight her mum had sorted for us. We were off to Israel for ten days to do a yoga retreat in the mountains, a yoga retreat with a load of teachers who are well-practised.

The flight to Israel was five hours; I was proper shitting myself on the take-off and focused on Emma and her mum to take my mind off it. Emma all gorgeous with her pinky hair, big blue eyes, slim toned body with mad swag. Her mum Beverly is so buff, mid 50s and super attractive. Strong, with her bobbed black hair, stunning features, she walks like a queen in the urban jungle.

When we arrived it was warm – it was the end of April, 2013. Spring had started late that year, pretty much the week we got there, thankfully, as it had been a long, hard and very cold winter. Palm trees lined the motorway. We were picked up by Vered, one of the Yogis on the course. Although it's sandier than the UK, there's lots of green in Israel. The houses are pretty, mainly one-storey; more wide than tall.

Vered welcomed us into her home and we were fed a feast of olives, falafel, cheeses, salad and love. Her home was warm: her heart heated the house. We slept well that night, ready for the journey the next day. We woke early to do a little chant then set off on our way to the course. We played Outkast as we sped down the motorway. I absorbed the whole journey. I felt at home in this new sandy land.

We stopped for food and a coffee at a small cafe on a mountain. The view from the café was breath-taking, an endless landscape of mountains. Surrounded by the wisdom of the mountains, we sipped on drinks in the valley. The vastness of life filled my soul with a healing glow: I was excited to be on the journey, if not quite sure how I got there.

We were staying in a Kautz, which is a community that lives together in the mountains – a self-sufficient community made up of lots of families. They had a big canteen like in a school, and halls that could be rented. Emma and I shared a room with two single beds. We had a bathroom, and a sink next to the kettle and fridge, kinda like a small studio apartment with a room and windows, standing on its own though, not piled up into the sky like I was used to in London. It was a small space, but our space.

After we had dropped our bags, we went straight into the hall to start the practice. We began with a silent meditation. I had no idea we were even gonna meditate. I had never meditated silently in my life. I tried to a couple of times when I was a teenager but couldn't get my mind to stop thinking, so it didn't work too well. I felt so uncomfortable, and a bit pissed off that

I didn't know we were gonna be meditating as I didn't enjoy that. I sat cross-legged. Somehow Emma's mum had made sure me and Emma were right in front of the teacher. The mats were placed in a semi-circle in rows: we were centre-front row, but not totally up in the teacher's face.

My mind started wandering. I was trying to keep my eyes closed and be good at meditating but I would open my eyes, look around, then close them again, trying to carry on meditating. Then my mind started to play movies, films of my life. Suddenly it would flip out of one film into another one. I would try to remember the first film but the second film would be playing and I couldn't make my mind go back.

Then I realised I was deceiving myself, making up stories to fill the time and keep my mind occupied. I wished I could fall asleep. My body hurt from sitting in position, and when I moved my legs about, tears streamed from my eyes from tiredness, but I couldn't fall asleep.

Meditation finally finished, and we went straight into a two-hour yoga class. I was not prepared for this, either. My mind was bitching and moaning all over the place. We were in a hall with wood flooring. It was quite a humble building. The windows behind the teacher had the most glorious green plants behind it, inhabited by birds singing a welcome song just for us. But I couldn't find the joy in the moment. My complaining arse was still annoyed at the meditation. My body did need the movement, though. When we finally got to the end of the class we lay in Savasana for 15 minutes, which is the lying-on-your-back pose. That's so long!

Dinner was gorgeous in the canteen and I did feel calmer after it. We ate lots of salad – the place did buffet-style food, so you could go back as many times as you wanted to. That night we slept well.

The morning started off with silent meditation until 12pm, when we would stop for lunch. Emma and I decided to take it very seriously. We rose at 6am to reach the hall for 7am, and started with one hour of silent closed-eye meditation: it was serious torture.

It was a little chilly in the mornings there and took a while to get our muscles warmed up. The first morning that I started to get into the meditation, I could feel my heart and it hurt – it hurt with pain connected to my dad and brother: I had fallen out with my dad and brother after Dad had falsely informed us that he had cancer before I flew out. I breathed into the space, filling it with light and talking to an inner me, letting myself know that it was OK. I visualised healing with my brother and Dad during the meditation and my heart started to lighten up.

That moment seemed to last forever. When it ended, we did 20 minutes of flicking open our eyes, nostrils and moving feet and hands. After that, we did 20 minutes of breath work, clearing the lungs of all air, then balancing the chakras and the left- and right-hand side of the body.

There was a break at 9am. Emma and I took the no-talking very seriously and ignored everyone who tried to talk to us. We had a snack of a handful of nuts. The sun illuminated the grass, and there was hope in the air, the promise of brighter days after the winter. The grounds were beautifully kept – a groundskeeper looked after the flowers as we sat and pondered life.

After the break we went into a two-hour practice. It was a slow yoga, no astanga jumping about the place; the pace was for the patient, and I wasn't quite sure I could reach that space in myself, but I did my best. There were women there in their sixties who could balance their whole bodies on their forearms: I watched them in awe as I caught the green of the trees that peeped through our windows. I was surprised my monkey mind didn't make a home in the branches, the way it was swinging about.

Our teacher, Orit, was a little wizard: a small woman aged about 55 I reckon. She wasn't a slender yoga babe; in fact she looked a bit like a hedgehog. She had wavy brown and grey hair past her shoulders, I think, but I couldn't really see 'cause she kept it tied up. She had very wide hips, like a spectacular riverbank that holds a river. She flowed like the water, effortless in her postures. Behind her little round glasses she didn't give much away. She spoke slowly and wanted silence in her class. I was kinda prang of her: I put her on a pedestal. I think that came from church days and worshipping teachers. She was mad cool though. I didn't catch her eye or say hello.

When we took a break and went outside, the weather had turned hot. We were there with women in their 40s, 50s and 60s and they were all babes. Everyone stripped and sun-bathed on the grass as we had a three-hour break during the day. The locals didn't like us much; the English with their sexy bodies out on the lawns. There were families in hijabs close by – it was a culture clash and we were not from there and I was conscious of it.

I enjoyed being with strong confident women. These women had been through it, but were not defeated by life; they had used their practices to shine. Emma and I were bonding, loving life and doing our best in the workshops.

After lunch we went straight into a half-hour silent meditation. It was my worst meditation of the day. My eyes watered and I just wanted to be done with it. I would wait for the little bell to ding: it was torture to listen to my own mind. I would rather do anything else. Nevertheless I sat there, legs crossed, eyes streaming, getting on with it.

Dinner was lovely – a good hour-and-a-half break back at the canteen for the buffet. Queueing with our trays, the bright canteen lights along the long tables gave it a feeling of being in the school dinner queue. I felt a little awkward to talk to anyone, 'cause I thought I was less spiritual or something lame like that, my ego getting in the way of connection.

We meditated for another half an hour in the evening, then studied old Sanskrit texts in groups, old Indian yogi philosophy, making notes to share back as a group. By the end of the day I was fucked: we started each day at 7am and finished at 9pm, did two-and-a-half hours of silent meditation, four hours of yoga, one hour of breath and body balance, and an hour of study. My lazy body and mind tried to fight the process but I had to surrender.

*****

Each day we focused on different postures, working into them very slowly. I was used to showing off in yoga class, jumping about like a jumping jack, but here I was struggling. There were no mirrors and it took as long as necessary. This was a whole new way of learning, in this humble hall set in magnificent grounds in the Israeli mountains.

One morning I was really struggling with the positions where I had to balance on my hands. I had pain in my right hand, and was having trouble putting my hand down flat on the mat. During savasana at the end of the class, I remembered the accidents I'd had with my thumb when the car boot was slammed on my foot and then I fell off the bike while I stayed at Uncle X's in Ireland when I was ten, the pain I had been carrying and the fear attached to it for over 20 years. I had had so much shoulder and neck pain on that side of my body over the years: it's crazy how the body will store pain. I worked through the issue in the meditation; I visualized the healing in my body taking place; I tried to open my heart to forgiveness with my Uncle. All this was so super new, healing myself; going on such a deep inward journey.

The sun blazed a perfect heat and the blue sky seemed endless, with minimal clouds. The grounds were so beautiful. My heart danced as it caught sight of the beautiful flowers, absorbing the vibration and wisdom of the Israeli mountains. I wanted to get close to Orit, our teacher, yet I was scared to talk to her. I don't know if this was some leftover stuff from Christianity or from school, where teachers seemed godly or out of reach. She didn't speak much and was kinda strict, so I kept my distance until I was ready.

One of the women I was in the evening study group with asked if I had had the euphoria in the meditation. I was like, 'What euphoria?' I was going straight into the realms of hell of deep healing and reflection in each meditation. I couldn't get out of my physical body.

One morning at 7am, wrapped in a blanket 'cause the little hall was cold, I felt as if my mum had jumped into my body and she was healing a part of me. Those meditations were super trippy.

Emma and I had such a good time sharing a room; I would leave her love notes in the morning 'cause we didn't talk until 12pm each day. One morning we met up with the group to have a meditative walk, where you walked really, really slowly, enjoying each step. The walkway was picturesque, lined with trees with newly budding spring flowers. The air was crisp. Luckily Emma's mum was as bored as I was and we walked on ahead at a good speed. We walked to the end of the kibbutz, where there was a mountain landscape in front of us; the magnificence of this planet revealed to us.

We made friends with a big bouncy dog that came over to play: he had long fur and loved a big hug. I was fully glowing, inside and out. I spoke with Emma's mum that morning – not about much – but as the sun came up over the mountain in the distance I felt hopeful; I felt peaceful.

That morning during the meditation I felt the euphoria: tears of gratitude flowed down my face landing on my chest and everyone in the room was beautiful; even the woman with a grey moustache. I could see the beauty in everyone and everything. My heart felt bigger than the room. The birds sang for us as they did every morning, but today, it felt like the ode to joy. I felt like I had double dropped some Es, but without the sweaty palms or my jaw swinging: this love was real; the chemicals in my brain had produced it.

At lunch, I put my arm around the teacher, Orit, and told her I was a poet and had a new poem I would like to share with her on the night of the final sharing. Orit looked at me and said a little abruptly, 'Can I at least get my lunch first?'

Feeling a little foolish for my timing and the urgency, I was still glad I had the bravery in that moment and jumped on it.

The last evening – that Friday – Orit invited me to stand in her space and share my poem with the group. In my mind I was thinking, WHAT THE FUCK, allow it: I can't stand in the space of the teacher. Why was she even offering that up to me? I stood in her spot, shared my heart and soul in the form of a poem and the group erupted in applause. Emma sang a song, then we performed together with a guitarist that we had been rehearsing with over the lunch break. It brought a warmth to the evening. I thought the performance would have been a lot less formal, not all of us in the form we held during the class, still with the yoga mats out. There was my bravado again; leading me into situations I then had to stand in.

We fed for the night and met around a fire. The flames danced a song of freedom while a kitten played at my feet. The people in the group I hadn't spent much time with became friends that night. We were a family of yogis, the fire keeping us warm. We sat on logs with the trees as our shelter. Our Mother Earth held us in her power with her strength. The sky was full of stars, a blanket that twinkled magic into the night.

We had one last morning of meditation and practice, then we had lunch and left the mountains. On the way back in the car, along the dusty roads which lined with mountains, I wondered why there were McDonald's signs by the roads. Out here in nature the signs stuck out like glitches in the Matrix; was anything sacred any more?

*****

We said goodbye to Vered then jumped on the train to Tel Aviv. The train was like a double-decker bus, which was super exciting. We arrived to be greeted by another one of Beverly's friends, who took us to her home. We were in another kibbutz, which is a collective community, this time by the sea. She had a partner and four children. We had gone from the quiet mountains to a busy household. I got a working WhatsApp connection on my phone and was able to communicate with everyone back home. In the retreat I had had very minimal wifi.

The beach outside was picturesque, without a soul in sight. The pathway that wound down to the shore was lined with tropical plants. I was in heaven in this moment. We had a long walk down the beach, just me and Emma. We chanted to the sunset. The red sky promised a beautiful day the next day. We sat silently after the chant, the sun filling our bodies.

We had a full family dinner then went to bed on the floor, which was a fun adventure. They were such a gorgeous family, moving rooms to make space for us. The ten-year-old stayed out late at a beach party – he was allowed to come home alone at midnight as it was safe in their community and he was with the other children. The mum of the family worked at the nursery in the community; the dad was in construction. The children were happy, healthy and had plenty to do.

The window shook with a rumbling sound, and we were told that they were testing bombs nearby and that it was nothing to worry about. The oldest girl, who was almost 18, was looking forward to being in the army. I thought, why do you have to go into the army? But in Israel all kids serve two years in the army when they reach 18 years of age.

The three days there were a perfect end to the experience: we ate out, explored the nearest city and swam in the sea. We had nourishing family time, laughter, hugs, great conversation and very good food.

It was time to go back to London. The trip had changed my life. I went back, determined to get into my Buddhist practice so much deeper, 'cause I could understand now that when I supported another person, I was supporting my own life; that the rhythm of supporting others in faith is powerful; it jolts me out of my pain and ego and connects me to the infinite power of the universe.

SGI

Lena, my best friend of around 15 years, introduced me to Buddhism. Back at her mum's, when we were in our early twenties, we would pass her mum in the living room with a low hum coming from the door. Lena was like, 'She sounds like a bee!' I was like, 'Yeah, a bee.' I didn't think much more of it at the time.

I moved in with Lena from 2007 to 2009 and during this time Lena had started to practise Buddhism. She was in the room next door to me. I would be high on Coke at 10am while Lena would be doing her hour-long morning practise. I would be thinking allow it, being all healthy and happy: I'm here tryna be high and fucked up. Her daily routine highlighted to me my lack of any routine at all, my constant state of not caring much to what happened in my life.

We met some new friends Emma and Tricia from the music scene and started to hang out with them. We had a party one night and Lena brought out her Gongyo book. The girls knew their prayers and were vibing and bonding over Buddhism. I did not want to connect at all; my inner being was wincing at the light so I poured myself another drink and kept the party going. Emma and Lena would sometimes chant together. I was kinda jealous as I didn't want my friends hanging out without me, yet I weren't ready to do this thing they were into.

I met Lena for a walk on Hampstead Heath one August afternoon. The temperature was perfect to be able to really enjoy the day, and the green of the park soothed my soul. The walk opened up my life: Lena spoke of her friend Rosie who had transformed her life thanks to her Buddhist practise. Rosie is an ex-addict. At that time I didn't want to admit that I was an addict; something in me must have resonated with her story though, and I said yes to chanting at her house that week.

I arrived on the Friday, at the small flat in Tufnell Park, a cosy living room with soft carpet and people chanting. Rosie let in guests who were flowing through the flat all day. I was given a Nam Moyho Renge Kyo card and I repeated the mantra with the others in the room. For an hour I went deep into the chant, with a focus on healing family Karma: I felt the call to the universe. Nam Myoho Renge Kyo, the mantra of the title of the last 28 chapters of the Lotus Sutra that we chant, means I devote my life to the mystic law recognising the manifestations through the symantaity of cause and effect.

The next week I stayed at Lena's as her mum was in Ireland and she was living closer to where I was working for the week. We chanted every morning while I was learning Gongyo. On the Friday Lena came downstairs and said, 'Let's chant.' I didn't want to though – I had chanted all week and on this day I just weren't feeling it at all. The phone rang in the middle of Lena doing the prayers. My dad was on the other end. He said, 'Shauna, it's about Mum.' I knew instantly what he was going to say, so I said it first: 'Mum died.' He replied, 'Yes.'

Fuck. How could this happen right now? I had a delayed response. The tears were yet to flow. My phone started to pop off, people calling me from all over the world; the word spread fast. I felt hollow. Emma came by that night to comfort me. She held me in bed while I sobbed my heart out, the pain was beyond any physical pain I had ever felt. My heart was in pieces. I felt sick and I couldn't eat; I felt totally disconnected, like I was under the sea and air weren't reaching my lungs.

The morning after the night before, the reality that she was gone and that this was now my life hit me. I chanted with Lena and I felt my mum's soul speak to me. She said that she was sorry for all that had happened between us. I forgave her and also said sorry for not being in contact for the past three years. It was her: her soul was close to me; I could feel her. She was in many spaces at once, the expansiveness that follows leaving your body.

The days were long and the grief was thick. As I was still staying at Lena's for a couple of weeks, I would pop over the road to join Rosie and her partner for the morning chant. Chanting was the only thing that would have my head surface from the sea of depression and desperation that was now my new costume.

I went back home to where I lived in south London during that time. I would walk to the Brixton centre, a centre owned by the SGI, where members and non members can pop in to chant in the evenings and weekends. People can become members at the centre as the ceremonies are held there. It was a good 40-minute walk to clear my head and heart before hitting the centre for an hour of diamoku (Nam Myoho Renge Kyo repeated) then back home. Nothing made any sense. I couldn't eat or sleep much for two weeks. Chanting gave me a brief glimpse of the Shauna I knew before I lost Mum.

I moved into Mum's old flat, which was one of the most painful and depressing decisions I have ever made. Yet a very necessary one, an Aunty had called and said Shauna, this will break your heart but you have to do it. Moving to Mum's after she passed was my opportunity to get a council flat, to finally settle down, get a home. Beautiful Lena would cycle down the hill on certain mornings and chant with me and the girls who lived at the flat. We would do a good hour. I didn't chant much on my own in them days. The Young Women's leader for the area, Ann, would often invite me over for morning chants at her place and a good talk after. Ann looked after the young women in the area local to her and I was one of the young women in her area. Those times I found it hard to wake up in the morning after long drink and Coke binges; my life was dark but those moments chanting gave me brief glimpses of hope like a shard of light through a dark cloud, a promise that the sun was behind the clouds, the wind would blow them on in time: but until then the grey was real.

I finally got my council flat a year later when I downsized from my mum's place. It was the perfect home to practise in. I was about to receive Gohonzon, which is the scroll we chant to, but I didn't have a Butsadan, which is the box we put it into. One of the members offered me hers. I walked in the pouring rain up to Cally Road, as I didn't have any money for transport. I picked up the box and went back to my place, and the next day I became a member of the SGI and had my own Gohonzon in my living room.

The days felt never ending with grief that had a hold of my soul, suffocating my life. I couldn't chant every day. I was still drinking very heavily and using Coke, Ecstacy and other chemicals to move me out of my desperate state of being. I would get fucked up, then once I would come down I wouldn't be able to chant. I would look at the Butsadan with the door closed: I couldn't open the doors to my life, the door to my happiness. I would look at the closed doors, which represented so much as I retreated into my withdrawn space. I would be able to chant some days and some days not. Sometimes I would not be able to move for 4-5 days at a time, in a very deep deperession. Sometimes I could get up and be motivated. It was so crazy, I wanted my life back, but when I got sucked back all I could do was ride it out.

I joined my local district with a Buddhist I knew in Mornington Crescent. It is a group of local men and women who chant then discuss topics together in the same area. Guests can attend the meeting. Our district was such an awesome eclectic mix of Buddhists: we had fashion designers, pensioners, gay people, straight people, publishers, mixed ethnicities, mixed aged groups and social backgrounds. Each month we discussed a topic based on the philosophy of our practise, topics such as 'winter always turns into spring': this is a metaphor looking at struggles we face in life and knowing that the winter of our life – the suffering – will always turn into the spring of hope. Our chanting opens our minds and hearts to receive the teachings and to make new causes in our lives.

I felt like I was 20 people all at once. In moments I could grasp this profound practise and in others I was living in hell, especially with heavy drinking and drug use. After two years of practise, which was more like a fire blaze up than a flow of water practise, I gave up drinking alcohol. One night my higher self, my Buddha nature spoke to me and asked me to stop drinking. I had planned to challenge myself to a year without drinking, so I thought why not, let me see what I can achieve in this time. It was not an easy decision: this was a lonely painful time, a time where I saw where my life really was at, the illusion my ego had created for me had been stripped bare. Naked in the mirror I saw I was out of shape in all areas of my life. Struggling with work, having to sign on, living without taking action for the life that I knew I could lead. If only I could get out of bed in the morning.

There were days when it felt like my body was made out of lead. Procrastination was how I spent my mornings. I would feel so anxious about chanting that I would push it back, then I would finally manage to chant just before 12pm. I then realised the work that I needed to do I could get done in a much shorter space of time if I chanted in the morning. Doing so cleared my mind. I gradually developed a new routine of chanting then getting my work done.

During the discussion meetings for the first couple of years I found it such a challenge to sit in a room for an hour and have a conversation that flowed between people taking turns to speak, my mind was so loud, jumping about the place. Without drinking and Coke binges I could feel how I really felt – and that was low. I made constant judgements of others, it was hard to hear new opinions, to really hear others and to accept them for who they are. This is part of my training in the SGI, learning though relationships and connections.

I weren't so trusting of the SGI at first. I kept thinking, who's this bunch of people who are happy all the time? I didn't believe it could be real. I didn't believe that such 'nice' people existed. I was resistant to joining activities and getting involved. Why would I want to give my time to the organisation, these people asked for too much. I gradually softened though, and started to open up to the kindness life was presenting me with.

I became a Young Women's district leader, contributing to the planning of the discussion meetings and supporting the other young women who practise in our district. I would chant with them in the mornings or the evenings and we shared each others' struggles, setting study and chanting targets to overcome issues and dramas in our lives.

We have a dedicated group called Lilac, this a group for the young women in the orginisation with the opportnity to support the local centre. The young women wear a navy blue suit with a white shirt and a red neck scarf. My first uniform was with some massive oversized trousers a white shirt I had had for around 10 years, which somehow survived my hectic schedule of travelling all over the place, year after year. I didn't see much point in getting a good uniform, I would rather buy clothes that I felt reflected who I am. I enjoyed our monthly study meetings and often held them at my home. Gradually I understood the purpose of the uniform, to work behind the scenes, to give without looking for an instant reward, I eventually bought a nice uniform and wore it with pride.

It was a year into the training at my local centre when I had just finished recording the album with the LC Collective and I thought I needed a whole day to rest now that I had finished. I woke that morning with the feeling that a ton of bricks were on my body. I had to summon some real energy from inside to move as I was to supporting the centre for the afternoon. By the end of the activity I felt light; my heaviness was to do with the darkness I was fighting from within. The time at the centre that day, holding open doors for others, giving to others, not only thinking of how I felt. By supporting others to find their happiness at the centre I tapped into my happiness. I left my activity that day, joyful with a massive smile on my face.

My life has grown alongside my practise: my event Lyrically Challenged went from being a smallish poetry event to a 350-people two-floor inspirational hip-hop event. I had put out a mixtape with the girls; I had a stable job working as a youth worker. Appeared on the Live Lounge for BBC Radio 1Xtra which was pretty awesome. Things were moving forward – not at lightning speed, at a slow and steady pace. If I didn't stop and appreciate all that I was achieving I might have thought I weren't making any movements at all.

I joined the Lilac team on a national level, supporting activities at Taplow court which is our national centre in Maidenhead. My life was full of fear then. I was so broke that I didn't understand why I would want to pay the £12 to get there, and why I would do it in the first place, getting up at 6am in the dark when I was feeling fucked and trekking all the way there? This provided an opportuntiy to look at my relationship with money, to deal with my poverty consciouness. To spend on supporting my life to reach where I wanted it to be, back in the day I would empty my bank account for a binge on drugs. Now I was contrubiting to an energy that supported my life. Meeting the most incredible young women on the way to and from activies, the conversations so solution focussed. I made friends for life, soul sisters in faith.

It is like a utopia at Taplow, the energy is serene, like a magical Buddha land, where the Buddhas meet to charge up and exchange ideas, inspire each other. I would be in a corridor to greet members and my mind would be talking so loudly to me. My mind was an absolute bully, it constantly put me down. I obsessively went over events from my past, looking at where

I thought I had gone wrong and what I was doing wrong in my life now. No wonder I found it hard to function when my internal dialogue was so harsh. I felt awful and exhausted at the end of the day. The poison of my life was seeping through my veins.

The activities created an opportunity for me to see how my mind was working and the effect this had on my daily life. It created an opportunity for me to redevelop my identity, to serve and support others. This was fundamental in the transformation of my lifestyle, I stopped using drugs, on a Saturday or Sunday morning I would be up bright eyed, fresh and ready to be at the centre. I used to still be high from the night before on a Saturaday and Sunday morning. My life had a deeper purpose now, I no longer felt the need to get wasted.

The practise teaches us how to transform our sufferings into peace and comfort; it's not an eradication of what is in your life, rather a light switched on so you can see the same life with new eyes. Through it you can see challenges and obstacles as opportunities for growth, and view all life as a benefit not begrudge circumstances as they are the perfect circumstance for our growth. These teachings are so simple yet can be so profoundly difficult to put into practise, particularly the concept of fully taking responsibility for all of my life, the good the bad and the ugly. My outer world is a reflection of my inner world; I only want to believe in these concepts when all is going well, when the joys of life are reflected back at me. When the shit is hitting the fan, I want to duck from that one and not look at how I created that reality. It is empowering yet confrontational to really look at my life, to be the one to make the changes by being the change I wish to see.

I could grasp concepts and then fall right back into the same old habits. Fall into depressive states, negative thoughts. Ahh, life you little trickster. As I started to study, supported by the members, I learnt not to begrudge my life. My sister and I would have unconstructive conversations in the morning for an hour on the phone, I would judge her for where her life was at and feel powerless to support her out of the situations she was in. Now instead I offered to come round and chant for an hour each morning, supporting her life as she was supporting my growth. We grew together. We got out of our moaning about life converstions, to empowering each other.

My leaders had been there through every step of this journey. During times of crises they stepped up and were by my side. I chanted for healing with Simon my mum's ex as this ghost was haunting my waking life. A couple of days later I had two wisdom teeth out; I ended up getting a dry socket and infections. As it was leading up to the weekend there was no action I could take to ease the pain; I had never felt pain like this before. Pain killers barely scraped the surface, I hadn't eaten, couldn't numb myself with shit TV. I knew I had to face it. I got some strong pain killers then did an SOS to my leaders.

The next morning I went to chant at Ayakos place, an older member in Camden. I chanted and within seconds I was in floods of tears. I felt so ashamed. Then I fell asleep on her sofa, I had let go and was vulnerable. She then came to my place later that day, I chanted half an hour with her then had to sleep. She carried on chanting while I slept. Then the women's leader came and chanted with me the next day for an hour. She sat behind me, strengthening me when I had no life force. The next day I got what I needed for my teeth and I was on the mend. The support helped me to heal my life; there have been countless times I have been supported in such a hands-on capacitiy.

I started to trust life again, to trust people as I had met genuine humans that really were invested in making sure that I was ok. I had not had this growing up, there had been so many let downs and I was shut off in so many ways.

To become a Buddha you do not become enlightened alone, you can only grow in faith through sharing this practise with others too, believing in the good in others. To grow to understand that every person has Buddhahood it just needs to be revealed, every life has potential. It can be easy to dismiss the potential in our fellow humans. I can want to ignore the person in front of me 'cause I want to be healed and to stand on my mountain of happiness alone. This is not happiness, though, because if my people are suffering then I am suffering: this is a principle of life. We are all connected: the illusion is that we are separate. We can't jump off the planet; every thought deed and action impacts the whole, the butterfly effect. We are profound; the change in a human heart can change the destiny of human kind.

I had the opportunity to see myself in a new light, to see who I was, the kind sides, the positive. When I made mistakes, a leader would visit to see how I could be better supported, I weren't told off or scolded. I then in turn took on more roles of responsibility and supported the younger in faith, young women in Camden.

I go to inspiration days, I support courses: I do it cause we are working towards world peace. Our mentor, Daisaku Ikeda, is a peace activist. He writes a peace proposal every year to the UN based on the abolition of nuclear weapons. But it is the weapons that we hold in our hearts that have them manifesting in our reality. My mentor has used his entire life to demonstrate the power of this practise based on the dignity for human life.

I can chant all day for peace then when confronted with conflict in my environment I then want to cut off and not remember the teachings. I have to check myself during my chanting sessions, to look at how I can respect another person's life in dialogue while also respecting my own. To reach a place where all parties feel heard and action is taken that benefits everyone. To think of peace on a macro scale I must be able to achieve peace on the micro that is my life. It's more than reading books and being able to have deep conversations, it is transforming deep-rooted behaviours and negative patterns that exist in my life. Then I can react and respond differently to everyone in my life: a human revolution in full effect.

By tuning into my mission, my life has opened up so beautifully. Becoming sober I am now the MC for the sober rave movement Morning Gloryville, jumping on the mic with Rudemental, Fat Boy Slim, Roger Sanchez to name but a few. Dancing with unicorns, mermaids, dancers and creatives in some of the best venues in the world. I was so afraid to become sober, it has lead me to spaces and communities that are more beautiful than I ever dreamed of. Chanting puts my life in rhythm with the universe, I connected with Samatha Moyo the founder of Morning Gloryville at a random party I almost didn't go to and became the resident MC. As I purified my life I moved away from doing jobs that didn't make my heart sing, I get to share my heart in some of the best parties I have been to in my life. Through the practise I become more and more who I really am, this manifests in work opportunites, realtionships and life.

Now I am working with young people in youth clubs, schools and Pupil Referal Units, sharing all I have learnt and my passion for life with the kids who are suffering the same fate I had growing up. The cycle is healing and we can make such a change when we are aligned to the best version of ourselves. I am conscious of how am I contributing to society now, what I have to give, and am sharing my life force for profound positive change on this planet, learning how to use my life and not just sitting and being swept along.

I contunie to go deeper into my practise while taking on responsibilities within the SGI, every responsibilities is an opportunity for growth. The orginisation is made up of human beings and no-one is perfect, yet being in an organisation where everyone chants, there is a lot of self reflection. We strive to be many in body and in mind with our mentor on the path to world peace, through the transformation of the human heart, one human heart at a time. A wonderful network of induviduals who work together for a transformation in society, a world free from war, a world where everyone is safe. I vow to my mentor to dedicate all my life to Kosen Rufu to use my life, all my life to demonstate the power of this practise, the power, of chanting Nam Myoho Renge Kyo.

"A great human revolution in just a single individual will help achieve a change in the destiny of a nation and, further, will enable a change in the destiny of all humankind. Diasaku Ikeda"

Letter to Mum After She Passed....

I read in a book about dealing with grief that it is good to write to the person that has passed away to process the emotions. Here is a raw piece I wrote for my mum.

To Mum,

I miss you and love you so much, I wish I would have found a way for us to get on in this life, and I wish that we didn't end on such bad terms. I believe your spirit knows how kindly and fondly I think of you. How grateful I am to have had you as my mum growing up. I know you didn't have much of a chance from the start.

Thank you for teaching me about the magic of the woods, how to climb trees the freedom of the branches. You were my perfect teacher in this university of life. I'm taking your lead and becoming a writer, because someone in our family deserves to get recognition for this gift we were all given.

I send a prayer to the angels to lift my anger and pain towards the past so I can be free and full of love. I ask for healing so that I can shine as I am meant to, to share messages that I channel in moments. I shine as I am meant to, born through a magical woman with 'the sight'.

Bless your soul; I love you more than I could ever say with these words in this book.

Love

Shauna xxx

Acknowledgements

I would like to say thank you to...

Lucie and the SGI UK for the support to transform my life

Nutty P for being my music producer and my councillor

All involved in Lyrically Challenged: Shay D, Sirena Reynolds, Emma Prior, Sonority, Eleanor Wilson, DJ Shorty

Reverie and DJ LaLa for the inspiration and friendship

My friends, Laura, Eloise, Sam, Lena, Brian, Lady MC, Jennie, Pixie, Tricia, Belle, Planetman, Mudge, The Rub, Phoenix, Bass 6

Red Jen for everything

Salena Godden and Kate Tempest
for the inspiration and support

Crystal Mahey-Morgan from OWN IT! for the belief in my vision and my writing and the whole OWN IT! team

My girlfriend Tash for the love and support

******

More Books from OWN IT!

PRISONER TO THE STREETS
By Robyn Travis

PRISONER TO THE STREETS

I learnt the hard way that you can't be *real* in something that's *fake* and you don't need walls around you to be IMPRISONED. This is the story of my life ON ROAD.

ROBYN TRAVIS

A real life account of Robyn Travis' journey to free himself from 'gang' life and 'postcode wars' in inner-city London and begin a new chapter in his life.

MAMA CAN'T RAISE NO MAN
By Robyn Travis

An explosive debut exploring notions of Black masculinity, single parent families and what is really means to be a man in today's society. An eye opening laugh-out-loud funny novel told through a series of prison letters

NO PLACE TO CALL HOME
By JJ Bola

With colourful characters and luminous prose, this is a tale of belonging, identity and immigration, of hope and hopelessness, of loss —not by death, but by distance— and, by no means the least, of love.

THE GROUP THERAPY PROGRAMME
By Various Artists

A multi-media digital book which tells the story of a fictional therapy session where a group of characters share how they are feeling through animated songs threaded together through an intra-animation.

WWW.OWNIT.LONDON

@OWNITLDN